The Illustrated Art Of Teaching Basketball To Your Children

By Bob Swope
2nd Edition 2004

Cover Photo
Courtesy of
Larry Hughes and his family
St. Louis University
And Photographer David Preston

Published and distributed by:
Jacobob Press LTD.
St. Louis, Mo.
(314) 843-4829

ISBN 0-9705827-6-5
Copyright 2002
All Rights Reserved
Including the right of reproduction in whole or in part in any form.

Printed and Bound by:
Hardbound, Inc.
St. Louis, Mo. 63031

First Edition 2002
Second Edition 2004

DEDICATION

This book is dedicated to my wife Jackie, who gave up many hours of companionship for me to write this book. And who encouraged me to keep going and not stop, even though she thought I was spending way too much of my time on the book. May god bless her because I love her very much.

AUTHORS ACKNOWLEDGMENTS

My thanks to the 6th grade boys basketball team and the 5th grade girls basketball teams, from St. Catherine Laboure parish in St. Louis, Mo. for all of their help. The pictures will really help illustrate what I am trying to get across to everyone using this book, to help children improve on their basketball skills.

BOYS TEAM- 2004

GIRLS TEAM- 2002

GIRLS TEAM- 2004

TABLE OF CONTENTS

1. **Warning**..6.

2. **Introduction**...7.

3. **Attitude Development**..9.

4. **The Fundamentals**..12.
   What are they..12.
   Centers..13.
   Point Guards...14.
   Shooting Guards...15.
   Small Forwards..15.
   Power Forwards..16.
   Organize your Teaching..17.
   Where they play on the court..17.

5. **Drills and Exercises**..19.
   How do they help...19.
   Warm up and Stretching...19.
   Coordination and Agility..25.
   Strength..27.
   Running..37.
   Quickness..38.
   Passing...40.
   Dribbling..45.
   Ball Handling...48.
   Catching...62.
   Faking..64.
   Footwork...68.
   Jumping..73.
   Shooting...75.
   Guarding..92.

6. **Defensive Techniques**..96.
   Man to Man, Guards..96.
   Man to Man, Forwards..100.

    Man to Man, Centers ....103.
    Man to Man Screens ....105.
    Man to Man Pick and Roll ....106.
    Shot Blocking, General ....107.
    Steals, General ....108.
    Man to Man Rebounding ....110.
    Diving for Loose Balls..112.
    Zone Defense, Guards ....113.
    Zone Defense, Forwards ....115.
    Zone Defense, Centers ....116.
    Zone Defense, Rebounding and Steals............................117.
    Other Zone Defenses ....117.
    Full Court Press Defense ....119.

7. Offensive Techniques ....120.
    Moving with the Ball, Guards ....121.
    Moving without the Ball, Guards ....123.
    Moving with the Ball, Small Forwards ....125.
    Moving without the Ball, Small Forwards ....126.
    Moving with the Ball, Power Forwards... ....126.
    Moving without the Ball, Power Forwards ....127.
    Moving with the Ball, Centers ....127.
    Moving without the Ball, Centers ....132.

8. Other Offensive/ Defensive Strategy Drills ....132.
    Defense during Free Throws ....133.
    Offense during Free Throws ....134.
    Breaking the Press on Offense...135.

9. New Parent Orientation ....138.
    The Game of Basketball..138.

10. The Offensive Game of Basketball..................................138.
    The Scoring of Points..138.

11. The Defensive Game of Basketball..................................139.
    Stopping the Opponents from Scoring............................139.

12. Other Phases of the Game...140.
    The Playing Rules..141.
    How the Players Line Up..142.
    Makeup of Teams..142.

13. The Playing Court Size...143.

14. The Referees..144.
    Why do we have Referees..144.
    Official High School Referee Signals..............................144.
    What they do...145.

15. Equipment..145.

16. Other available Sports Books......................................146.

17. Index...147.

* * * * * * * * * * * * **WARNING** * * * * * * * * * * * * * *

If your child or the participant has any physically limiting condition, bleeding disorder, high blood pressure, pregnancy or any other condition that may limit them physically, you should check with your doctor before participating in these drills and exercises.

Be sure participants, making hard contact, are of the same weight and size to avoid injury.

All drills and exercises should be supervised by an adult. **AUTHOR ASSUMES NO LIABILITY FOR ANY ACCIDENTAL INJURY OR EVEN DEATH THAT MAY RESULT.**

EXTRA CARE AND CAUTION SHOULD BE TAKEN WITH ANY OF THE VARIOUS PASSING DRILLS, AND SOME DRIBBLING DRILLS AS THEY ARE THE MORE DANGEROUS ONES.

Introduction

Some of my children and friends have been asking me to do a Basketball reference book for young boys and girls for some time now. The reason I am doing this now is, for them and all the young parents out there that can use the guidance. Also 2 of my grandchildren are playing basketball now, so this is for them. It has that certain appeal for me because when I was at this young age, of 5 to 12 years, there were no books out there for my dad to refer to, so he could help me. He was not into athletics much since he came from an era when men started to work at a young age, and I guess he never thought about sports. I really didn't start into basketball until I was maybe 13 or 14 years old. And even at that I kind of got into it because my friends were playing at the Jr. High School. When I really got into basketball was when my son wanted to play, at about 11 years old. His friends at school said there was a local league we could join if we came up with enough players to start a team. Well my son got enough kids to make a team, but they didn't have a coach. None of the kid's dads were interested, or knew about much about Basketball, so I volunteered so they could play. Since I had not played that much Basketball, I went to the Library and did as much research as I could. I was interested in Basketball since watching John Wooden's UCLA college teams play for years in Los Angeles while I was growing up. And so this is when I started to try and learn about Basketball. Our team was not very good, but I think the boys and me all learned some things and had fun. And through all of these years I have accumulated a lot of coaching reference material. And so with all my other coaching experiences, I am setting out to put together some guidance for young parents to use. I hope this will help their children learn how to play Basketball.

If you really analyze your sons or daughters, there is probably some niche in Basketball where they can find success. I might point out here that you can teach these skills to your daughters also. Many girls play Basketball these days, and these same fundamentals can help them as well as boys. On Saturdays we used to go out to this old baseball diamond, we had found over in an old abandoned farm area, and practiced Baseball for hours. My boys seemed to like it, so we tried to get over there every chance we had. As parents you can do this to, and have fun with your kids while they learn about Basketball.

A little history about me. I coached the one year of Basketball in Oxnard, California. I have been a Youth Football coach in Oxnard, California and in Gardnerville, Nevada for 6 years. I have been in the management of Youth Football in both places. Also I have been a baseball assistant coach and a manager.

I was an assistant coach in youth baseball in Oxnard, California, a manager and coach in CYC baseball in St. Louis, Missouri for 5 years. I also managed in CYC baseball in St. Louis. I have managed and coached mostly the very littlest boys, 7 to 10 years because my thinking is if you start them out with good fundamentals, those fundamentals will develop into long term habits. And most 7 or 8 year old kids will soak up just about anything you say, especially if you make it fun.

Some things I would like to mention here. Before you do any of these drills and exercises, make sure your son or daughter is healthy and in good shape. Also make sure their eyesight is good. There are a number of reasons for this. When they are passing and shooting the basketball, it is very hard, they can get hurt if it hits them especially in the head area. Another area to be concerned about is getting poked in the eyes with fingers. When another player reaches out to try and block the shot, they could accidentally poke someone in the eye.

I have tried to keep all the drills and exercises simple, so they can be accomplished without expensive equipment. There are things you have around the house that can be used as coaching aids. As you go through the book you will find these tools pointed out to you. However, you need a basket to practice Basketball shooting. In years past, I have heard of kids nailing a peach basket on a barn wall to use as a basket. I hope you don't have to resort to this, but if you do it will work. If you own your home, or get the owners approval, you can get a basket kit to install above your garage door. For Condo owners they have portable baskets you can fold up and store in a garage when not in use.

So this book is dedicated to all those mothers and fathers who have a son or daughter, who think they might want to learn how to play basketball. Usually mom and dad would like to see them get outside more and get involved in sports, but they probably don't know what sport to get them into. Well if its basketball, this book is for you. And some of you single moms, maybe you have a son or daughter and would like to get out there and do something with them. But you just don't know how to go about it. All of you that are in this situation, you probably would like to get out there with your son or daughter, and help them learn more about how to get ready to play basketball. Most mom and dads don't know what they can do, to have some fun with their kids and teach them something about basketball while doing it. For all of you out there, here is a book you can use as a guide or reference manual on the fundamentals with pictures. Take it with you out to the yard, or driveway, and use it as you go about teaching and having some fun.

Attitude Development

Influence

Most boys and girls, from the age of _five through eight_, are very impressionable. Mom and dads influence can be important in their development, at this stage of learning. It is also important to teach young kids that basketball is only a game, and what is most important for them to realize is, to develop good sportsmanship. Explain that they should always try their best, and if they don't do well every time there is always another day. One of the things I have learned is that if something is worth doing then try to be the best you can be at it. I realize this is very hard for some young kids to learn. So, what I always told the kids on my teams was, have someone watch you to see what it is you might be doing wrong. Then that person should work with them, over and over, to correct these things. I explained to them that if they worked hard they would begin to see that they were getting better and better. If your son or daughter has a good attitude, this will usually be reflected to the rest of the kids on the team. In other words it can be contagious to everyone else on the team.

Their Improving

Part of improving your son or daughters attitude towards other players on the team, coaches, managers and referee's, will depend a lot on how you normally act. They will most often reflect your attitude towards these people. So, be very aware of what you say when they are present or nearby. Many times I have seen parents screaming from the sidelines at referee's, or another kid on the team when they make a mistake. Then, following your example, during practice your son or daughter will belittle one of their team mates or the manager. This is really just learned behavior from you. And as parents we have to be honest with ourselves, we are not perfect so why should we expect them to be. Think about it if a team has to rely on a referee's call, or a team being perfect to win the game, then maybe they didn't deserve to win. A parents bad attitude just makes things worse not better. My advice to you is just bite your tongue, so to speak, until you cool off a bit. Then you will find that you can have a lot more fun out there. So, please instruct them to get along with their team mates. Because if he or she is a better player than they are, they can help the whole team more by encouraging them rather than by belittling them. It will help in showing them how they can become a better player, like he or she is. This way the whole team gets better. And when that happens everyone has more fun out there. On one of my Baseball teams I had several boys that became good at this, and they had a lot of respect from the other boys, and it helped the whole team.

Respect

Explain to your son or daughter the roles of the referees, and the head coach. Only the head coach should question the referee when he believes that a there has been a mistake, or a rules interpretation problem. Or maybe the referee was just out of position to see what happened. When you teach your son or daughter respect for the rules, then you teach them respect for law and order later in their life. Remember the example you set by your actions may influence the way their life turns out. Many times, at the youth basketball level as a coach if you are reasonable with a referee, and ask him to consult with the other referee, he may even on occasion reverse his opinion. They may have had a better view of the play. What usually happens though when the players, coaches, and parents, start screaming and complaining about the call, he will favor the other team on anything that is questionable or close. In the long run it is better to just let the referee make his call. Then, after the game is over or the next day, go to your "head coach" and tell him why you think the refereeing was poor. Your head coach should then go to the head of referees, and explain the complaint. It might just be that the referee is inexperienced, new, or just doesn't understand the rules. But he will never improve if the head of referees does not know that he has problems, and then helps him correct them. Believe me, he probably never will change by your hollering and screaming at him.

Hustle

Hustle will improve your son or daughters attitude, and make the game better to watch. A little game you can play with your kids is, whenever you are working with them, say "Lets see how fast you can run up and down the court, maybe you can beat me". Then do it yourself as fast as you can, and afterwards ask them to try. Then no matter how fast he or she does it, say "Gee your almost as fast as me". Then when you see that they are getting faster, offer them some kind of reward, then take them to a movie on the weekend. He or she needs to be taught how to run fast. When substitutions are made, they will need to run on and off the court fast to speed up the game. When there is a lot of hustle the game goes faster, and mom that will sometimes get you home a lot earlier to start supper. I have personally proven to myself that in life hustling, at whatever your job is, impresses the boss also. So this can help them in life also, and you should explain to them this is why they need to learn to hustle. Life is a whole lot more fun when people step it up a few notches, not necessarily all the time, but when it is called for. You parents will be happy and proud to see this, and so will their boss later in life.

Health Habits

General Good Practice
    It is a very good idea to start your son or daughter out in life with good health habits. What we are talking about here is plenty of sleep, a good nutritious balanced diet, and timely exercise. What we mean by timely is, don't over exercise them a few hours before game time. Not being tired, or sick, will improve their mental outlook and attitude during the game.

    Just a few words here about dietary supplements. **DO NOT** let them take anything containing *"Ephedra"*. It is illegal now in high in most high schools, and it has some very serious side effects. Death being one. So why take a chance. Let them develop naturally for the long term.

    I have had boys come to a summer afternoon or early evening baseball game, really dragging their feet, so to speak. And after talking to them, I found out mom let them go over to a friends house all morning at their swimming pool. Swimming is a good workout, but not the day of a game. They need at least one days rest from any heavy exercise before a game. As training for a sport these days becomes more complex, the trainers, and strength coaches, have found that some exercises actually can be dangerous. So what I have tried to do is, find out the latest techniques, and tailor the exercises to fit young kids playing and practicing basketball.

    The game of basketball takes lots of stamina, to play at the same level all the way until the end of the game. In the last period they need a physical advantage going for them. To be able to do this, young kids need to work on their conditioning constantly. Not over do it, but keep at it every day for at least a few repetitions. If your son or daughter is on the overweight side, be extra careful not to over work them, or push them too hard. Especially when they begin to exercise for the first time. You only have them increase repetitions when you see that they are getting into shape, and can handle it. If there is any question, talk to your doctor about it.

    We tried all kinds of techniques, to help kids keep their strength level at or near its peak. Most teams go through a warm up exercise routine of some kind, just before the game starts, to get them loosened up. So don't worry about exercising them for the game. We had some boys, that appeared to loose stamina during the game, eat a banana the day before a game to let the vitamins get into their systems by game time. The idea there being, make sure these vitamins did not get all sweated out of their system during the game. Now days they have *"GatorAid"* for that.

A suggestion here would be, give your son or daughter some *"GatorAid"*, by taking a bottle with you when you are out working with them. Especially if its warm where you are practicing. We had one coach that had one of the parents cut up oranges, and hand them out to suck on during break. Both of these ideas helped some, but then when they came out with *"GatorAid"* that worked out much better when they are thirsty during practice or during a game.

Infectious Disease Control

Here are some rules to follow, with respect to infectious diseases being spread through contact with blood. This would be when a player, or even a referee, is bleeding. If the referee, or an official, notices that anyone on the court is bleeding, they should stop the game immediately. Or if you are a parent in the stands watching the game, and notice someone on the court bleeding, let an official know right away. The person bleeding should be removed from the game, for evaluation and treatment. If the player can not return, then a substitution can be made. If the player returns, the injury must be covered with a bandage, or cover of some kind that won't come off and expose the blood. If a uniform has blood on it, then it must be changed to a clean uniform. If the playing surface, ball, or other equipment, get blood on them, then the game should be stopped. And the area along with the equipment, should be cleaned. All of these precautions are taken to protect everyone, from coming into direct contact with blood that could be infectious.

The Fundamentals

What are they

Fundamentals are the basic skills needed to be able to play the game of basketball. The Basics are running, dribbling, shooting, passing, catching, jumping, and guarding. Even though it would be good to teach your son or daughter all of these, I am going to break them down into the different positions for you. The reason being that most boys and girls will not be able to master all of these basic skills or positions. If you can't, in your mind, figure out what position they might be good at, then teach them strength, speed, and coordination. They can always use these skills no matter where they play. As an example, if your son or daughter is very tall for their age, with a long legs on a thin frame, and comes from a tall thin family, they will probably end up being a center in youth basketball. And mom or dad, you will probably have to make the decision on what it appears they will become when they grow older. Try and imagine what position they might fit into when they get to high school age, and then match them up with the possible position examples we will give you. Look at your parents and see what kind of body structure they have. Moms, most of the time your son will inherit a similar structure to your father, and fathers most of the time your daughter will inherit a similar structure to your mother. You dads, whatever you do don't try to make them into a player at a position you always wanted to be in. Most of the time your son will take after his mothers side of the family, and daughters will take after the fathers side of the family. Dads you may be big and tall, but more than likely if your wife is smaller in size, your son will be smaller than you are. And mothers you may be big and tall, but if your husband is small, your daughter will probably be small also. Although these days there is always exceptions. Take this into account when you decide what to start training them as. As an example if your son or daughter is very small and fast, don't try and make him into a center. Maybe a playmaker guard would be better. The trick is, try and teach them a position they can succeed at. After a few years if it appears he is changing into a different size, skill level, or structure than you imagined, you can always teach him the additional skills he will need for another position. So, don't spend a lot of time trying to teach them how to be a center if he or she is going to end up a playmaker guard. Spend it more wisely on improving their strength, speed, and coordination at this young age.

Centers

The fundamental skills that centers need are strength, quickness, agility, jumping, and guarding. The center also needs to be coordinated, and a good athlete. In the chapter on ***"Drills and Exercises",*** you will find out how to teach them these skills. Make sure they have good shoes. With the pounding from jumping, and running up and down the court, they need protection for their feet. Probably the fundamental you need to concentrate first on is strength, then jumping, agility, quickness, and guarding last. If they do not have the strength to stay in the low post, and block out the opposing center, they probably just won't make it as a center because they will get pushed around. He or she has to have jumping ability to get up in the air, and grab rebounds off the backboard. Also they need to learn how to guard the basket, and block out. They are usually the tallest player on the team. If a potential center does not have agility, coordination, and quickness, they will probably not be able to master getting into position to block shots, or stop an opposing player from driving in for a lay up. So when you start out playing with him or her, take notice of their agility and jumping abilities. If they can, right from the start, move around fairly easily, and jump up high for balls off the backboard, then they might make a good center. They also need to have good shooting abilities. This is because when they are down on the offensive end of the court, they are usually counted on to make the basket. This is mostly because they are taller than most of the other players.

Point Guard

The fundamental skills point guards need are quickness, agility, dribbling, passing, stealing, shooting, and guarding. The fundamental skills you need to concentrate first on is dribbling, then agility, quickness, passing, stealing, shooting, and last guarding. This is because if they can't bring the ball down the court by dribbling, which is their primary job, they probably won't make it as a point guard. The point guard also needs to be smart. They should be the teams best passer and ball handler. And they are usually one of the smallest players on the team. They push the ball down court, and get the offense going. He or she will have to learn how to bring the ball down the court, look for the open person to pass to, or look for the center. For this reason they need to be able to dribble the ball without looking down. Also they have to give the signal for whatever play the coach wants to run. They have to be especially good at dribbling because if they are being pressed by an opposing player, as the ball is brought in down in their end of the court, they don't want that player to steal the ball away from them this close to the basket. This is very important down in their own end of the court. If the opposing player does manage to steal the ball, he might be able to go in for a quick lay up and score. On defense, they will also have to learn how to guard against the opposing guards bringing the ball up court. In the chapter on ***"Drills and exercises",*** you will find out how to teach them all of these skills. If a potential point guard does not have the ability to pass the ball quickly, and accurately, they probably won't make a good point guard. So when you start out playing with him or her, take notice of their dribbling and passing abilities, by testing them. If they can, right from the start, dribble and pass the ball fairly well, then they might make a good point guard. They do need to be able to shoot the basketball occasionally because if everyone else is covered they need to take the ball to the basket and score. Make sure they have good shoes and don't scrimp on price. With the constant running up and down the court, and the stress on their feet from jumping, their feet need good protection.

Shooting Guard

The fundamental skills shooting guards need are quickness, agility, dribbling. shooting, passing, and guarding. They are a lot like a point guard, except they are usually just a little bit taller, but shorter than a small forward. The fundamental skill you need to concentrate first on is shooting, then dribbling, quickness, agility, passing, and last guarding. This is because if they can't shoot good from the perimeter (three point circle), they probably won't make it as a shooting guard. They need to be the teams best perimeter shooter. They don't have to be great at handling the ball, but when they get the ball they must be able to shoot, pass the ball, or drive to the basket. Also they must be ready to grab any rebounds near them. To be a good shooting guard they must be able to come off of screens, and shoot. Speed and quickness is very important for them to learn, so they can dribble drive fast off of the screens. On defense, they will also have to learn how to guard against the opposing guards bringing the ball up court. In the chapter on ***"Drills and Exercises",*** you will find out how to teach them these skills. They are also sometimes known as the "two guard". They must learn how to have a quick release on their jumper shot. Since the three point shot has been introduced to the game of basketball, the shooting guard has become more important to the team. When you first start out playing with him or her, take notice of their ability to move around quickly, and can they make their shots. If they show at least a little natural talent to do these two things, then they might make a good shooting guard. Also a shooting guard has to learn to go to the board, for a rebound after shooting, where a point guard has to stay back, and defend against any fast breaks back up the court by the opposing team. Make sure they have good shoes because with the constant stress from running and jumping, their feet need good protection.

Small Forward

The fundamental skills a small forward needs are strength, shooting, jumping, quickness, agility, passing, guarding, and dribbling. The fundamental skill you need to concentrate first on is strength, then shooting, jumping, agility, quickness, passing, guarding, and last dribbling. This is because if they are not strong enough to get inside, and get in position to shoot, they probably won't make it as a small forward. They must also be able to learn how to shoot inside, or out on the perimeter, which is basically their job. They should be aggressive as well as strong, to be able to mix it up with the opposing player while getting into position inside. Even though they are taller, and usually not as quick as a guard, they must also be agile enough to handle the basketball, and pass when necessary. Since they have to play a lot inside, they have to be good jumpers, to grab rebounds. They should be too tall, too tough, and too aggressive, for a shooting guard to handle. On defense, they will also have to learn how to guard the perimeter, move quickly around screens, and stay with the shooters going to the basket. In the chapter on **"Drills and Exercises"**, you will find out how to teach them these skills. I personally believe that if you match their natural size, skills, and abilities, to this position then they have a very good chance to be successful. Since they play inside a lot, they get fouled a lot. So they will have to learn how to make free throws. Work with them on this. When you first start out playing with him or her, take notice of their aggressiveness and their ability to make shots. To test them, kind of lightly push them around a little bit, under the basket, and see what their reaction is. If they are at least a little aggressive from the start, and fairly agile, then they might make a good small forward. Don't forget about their dribbling because they do have to occasionally move around by dribbling. Also make sure they have good shoes because with all this jumping, and moving around they do, their feet need good protection.

Power Forward

The fundamental skills a power forward needs are strength, shooting, jumping, quickness, agility, passing, guarding, and dribbling. These are basically the same skills a small forward needs, except they need to have at least a little weight bulk to them. The fundamental skill you need to concentrate first on is strength, then shooting, jumping, agility, quickness, guarding, passing, and last dribbling. This is because if they are not strong enough to stay in position inside, to grab rebounds or score, they probably won't make it as a power forward. They have to learn how to take a pass and score in the lane (the paint area or free throw lane). They have to be strong enough to not let the opposing player push them out of their area. Also they need to learn how to guard the basket, and block out. Like the center, when passed the ball in an area of about 15 feet all around the basket, they are expected to score. In the chapter on **"Drills and Exercises"**, you will find out how to teach them these skills. Sometimes the power forward is known as "The Enforcer", or the "Four Spot". Since they play inside a lot, they get fouled a lot. So teach them how to make free throws. When you first start playing with him or her, take notice of their aggressiveness, and their ability to make shots. Again, to test them, kind of lightly push them around a little bit, under the basket, and see what their reaction is. If they are at least a little aggressive, and don't back off, and they can shoot under the basket, then they might make a good power forward. Also don't forget to teach them to dribble because occasionally they have to move around with the ball. They need to learn how to pass the ball off, and set up plays. Make sure they have good shoes because with all this moving around and jumping, their feet need good protection.

Organize your Teaching

To organize your teaching, have a plan. My suggestion is sit down, read the section in the book where I talk about how to determine what position your son or daughter might be good at. Then go through the rest of the book, and read the sections where I show the exercises, drills, and skills, needed for that position. As you go through the book, start a *list* of what they need to practice. Next to that particular drill or exercise, put down approximately how much time will be needed to accomplish the teaching and practicing. This way you can plan your teaching sessions. I am sure that when you get done, you will see that it takes a lot of hours to go through the fundamentals they need to learn. And with the few hours each week their coach has to go over fundamentals, time runs out, and they have to start working on plays and tactics. So teaching them from 5 years old, even a little each year, will really help them improve on their skills.

Where they play on the court

There are many different alignments on the court. The ones we show are generally where they play. To interpret the diagrams on page 18, use the following player identifications. The center is noted with a "C", the power forward with a "PF", the small forward with a "SF", the shooting guard with a "SG", and the point guard with a "PG". We will show typical defensive and offensive alignments.

OFFENSE

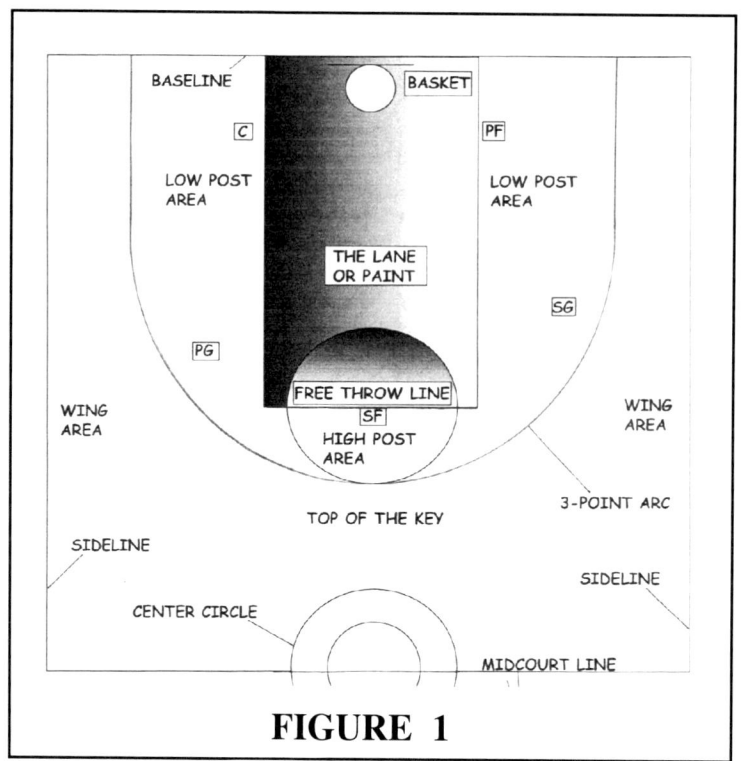

FIGURE 1

DEFENSE

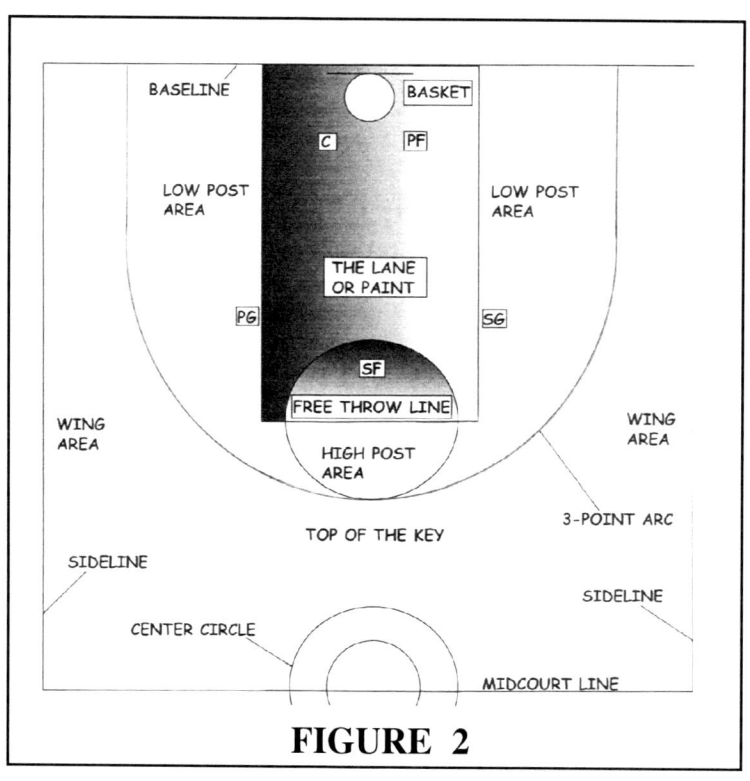

FIGURE 2

Drills and Exercises

How do they help

The drills and exercises in this chapter have been proven to help young boys or girls to improve their skills, to a higher level than they might achieve normally. I will break them down into the fundamental categories, and how they will relate to what you want to teach. We will use picture figures, and diagrams as much as possible, to eliminate some of the confusion for mothers, and some fathers, who may never have played the game of basketball. Several things I would like to point out here is, generally speaking up to the age of about 12, girls may be a little more coordinated. And in some cases they may be stronger than boys. The other is, the same fundamentals are needed for boys and girls at the young ages of 5 to 9 years. This is why I have put them all together in this book. So, bear with us those of you that have played a lot of basketball. This book was written as a reference book for moms and dads to use in teaching, and training, their sons and daughters the skills of playing basketball. You can take this book right out in the yard or driveway with you, to look at for reference. I might suggest here that if your son or daughter does not seem to be very interested in exercising, then try to make a game out of it. For instance say something to them like "I bet you can't do this better than me", or "I bet you can't beat me down to the fence". Then do the exercise, but run a little slower, and let him or her run a little bit ahead of you. Well you know what I mean.

Since a lot of my thinking and experience is so called old school, I will use a lot of the 1950's to 1970's basketball drills and exercises, but I am also going to add in some of the newer drills and exercises. Then I am going to throw in some football drills, which really help out with a young boy or girls agility and coordination.

Warm up and Stretching

Before any exercising jog slowly around the back yard, or wherever you are training, for a few minutes to make sure to get the muscles warmed up. This is absolutely required before you start any exercising. After warming up, go right into the following stretching exercises. However when you start stretching exercises, go slowly and don't rush them along because you are in a hurry. And when you finish all exercising, go into a "Cool Down", don't just stop altogether. Walk around slowly, relaxing while you walk, for about 2 or 3 minutes to cool down.

FIGURE 3

Exercise No.1- Trunk Twister

This is for stretching the waist and stomach muscles. From the standing position, with legs apart, have them put both hands on their hips. Then have them twist their entire torso 90 degrees, hold it for 3 seconds, and back, 5 times to the right. Relax for a few seconds between twists. Next have them twist to the left 90 degrees, 5 times, hold for 3 seconds, and then back. This can be increased as they get older or if they are a little overweight *(SEE FIGURE 3)*.

Exercise No.2- Seated Leg Stretch

This exercise is for stretching the hamstrings, and quadriceps muscles. From the sitting position, have them put both legs together and straight out in front of them. The toes should be pointing up, and the knees pushed flat to the floor. Next put both hands side by side, and touch them to your toes. Hold for 3 seconds and then back to straight up. Relax for a few seconds. While doing this exercise, keep the back as straight as possible. Do about 5 of these stretches. This can be increased a little bit as they get older, or if they are a little over weight *(SEE FIGURE 4)*.

Exercise No. 3- Butterfly Groin Stretch

This exercise is for stretching the inner thigh groin muscles. From a seated position, have them put both of their heels together in front of them. Next have them grab their right ankle with the right hand, and the left ankle with the left hand. Then have them use their elbows to push downward, putting light pressure on their knees, then push forward slowly. Hold that

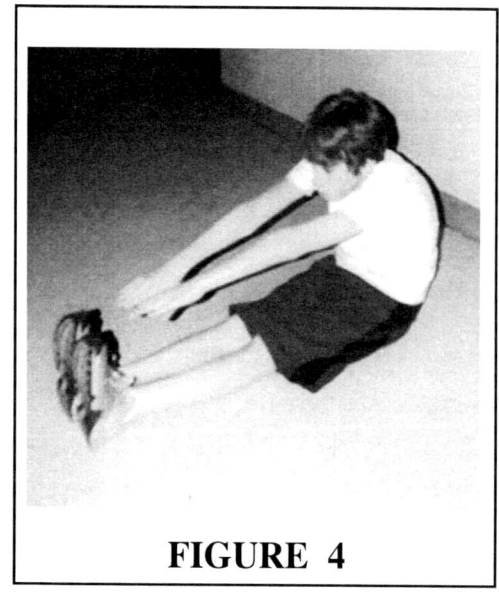

FIGURE 4

position for about 3 seconds, then relax for a few seconds. This exercise helps prevent groin pulls. Do this about 10 times. This can be increased a little as they get older, or if they are a little over weight *(SEE FIGURE 5).*

Exercise No. 4- Back Stretch

This stretching exercise is for the lower back and neck muscles. From the lying position, have them bring both legs up tightly to their chest. Next grasp both hands tightly together, at the top of the knees, with the neck raised up towards the knees. Pull down on the knees, and hold that position for 3 seconds. Then relax the arms and feet for 5-10 seconds. Repeat this at least 5 times *(SEE FIGURE 6).*

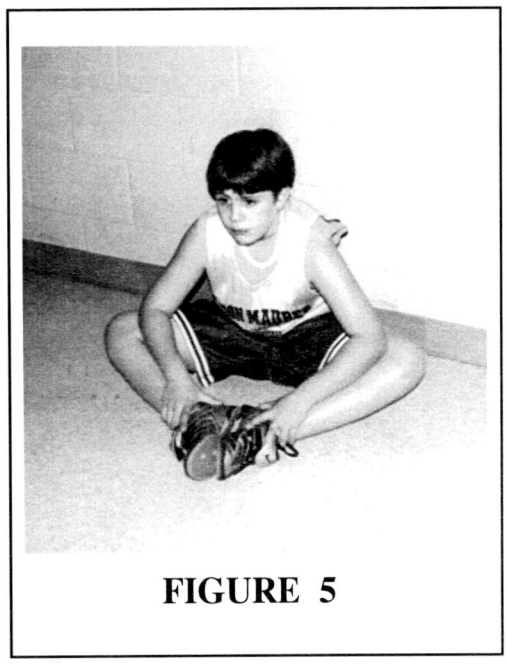

FIGURE 5

Exercise No. 5- Side Lunge Stretch

This exercise stretches the inside leg muscles, which they use when jumping for a rebound. Centers and power forwards especially need to do this exercise every day. Have them spread their legs from a standing position, so they feel a slight pull in their groin and hamstring muscles. Then have them bend over, and put both palms on the floor. Next have them lean to the left while bending the left knee, hold for 3 seconds, then to the right bending the right knee, and hold for 3 seconds. This is sort of like a slow delayed swaying motion. All the time keeping the palms on the floor in the same place. Start out by doing at least 5 of these to the left, and 5 to the right. As they begin to get more stretched out, you can increase the number, but remember to not over do it with them *(SEE FIGURE 7).*

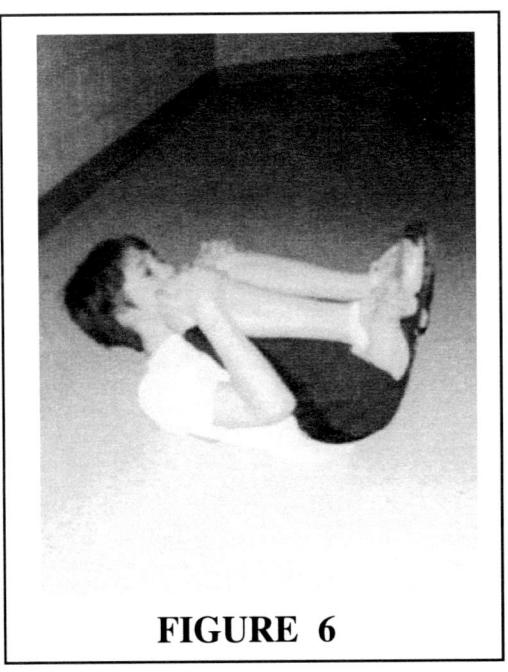

FIGURE 6

FIGURE 7

Exercise No. 6- Pelvic Twist Stretch

This stretching exercise is for the lower back, obliques, and gluteus maximus (behind). From the seated position, have them stretch both legs straight out in front of them. Then have them put their right leg over their left thigh, with the right knee pointing up, and the right foot on the floor pointing straight ahead. Next have them rotate their upper body to the right, so their shoulders are parallel to their left leg. Put the left elbow on the right thigh, and push down. Hold this position for about 20 seconds. Then switch arms and legs, and repeat the process to the left. Start out by doing at least 5 with each leg. After they have been doing these every day for awhile, you can increase the number slightly if you wish. Just remember they are kids, so don't get carried away *(SEE FIGURE 8)*.

FIGURE 8

Exercise No. 7- Kneeling Thigh Stretch

This stretching exercise is for the quadricep muscles. From the kneeling position, have them put the left knee down, and the right leg out in front with the knee bent. Put the right hand on the right knee, and the left hand on the left hip. Hold that position for 3 seconds. Relax for a few seconds, then switch knees and hands. Repeat this, so you do about `5 with each leg. After they have been doing these every day for awhile, you can increase the number slightly if you wish *(SEE FIGURE 9)*.

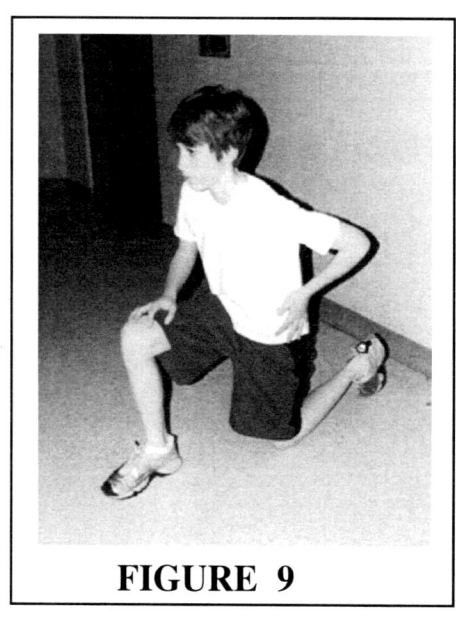

FIGURE 9

Exercise No. 8-Tricep, Lateral and Posterior Deltoid Stretch

This stretching exercise is for the arm, and shoulder area. Standing up, have them grab their right elbow, and pull it behind their head next to their right ear. Have them hold that position for about 3 seconds, then relax the arms for half a minute or so. They should feel a little pull in the back of their arm, on the tricep when they do this exercise. They should do about 5 of these with the right arm, then switch and do 5 with the left arm. After they have been doing these every day for awhile, you can increase the number slightly if you wish *(SEE FIGURE 10)*.

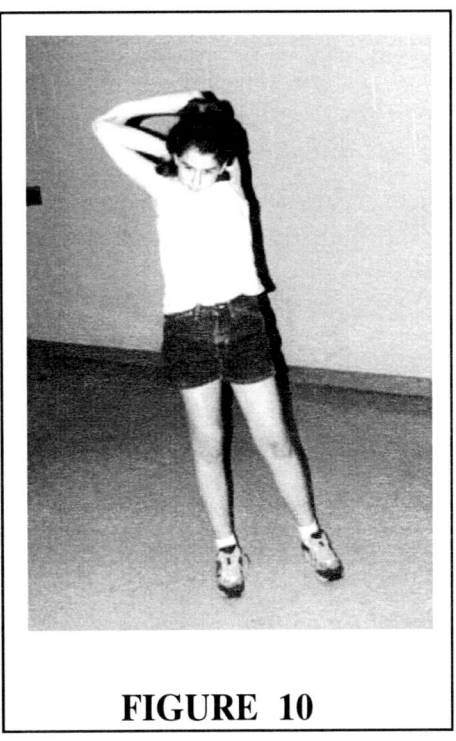

FIGURE 10

Exercise No. 9- Standing Calf Stretch

This exercise is to stretch the calf muscle. Have them stand up and stagger the left foot in front of the right, with both heels flat on the floor, and in front of a wall. Next have them lean forward and put their hands against the wall, then bend the leading front leg. They have to be far enough away from the wall, so they can feel the pull in their right leg. Have them hold this position for about 5 to 10 seconds, depending on how old they are. With 5 year olds at 5 seconds, and 12 year olds at 10 seconds. Starting out they should do about 5 of these with one leg, then switch and do 5 with the other leg. They can do a few more of them after they have been doing them every day for awhile, or if they are 10 to 12 years old. This will stretch out their calf muscles, which will help them with their sprinting, and running, for long periods of time. Also this exercise helps when you get a "Charley Horse" in your calf *(SEE FIGURE 11)*.

FIGURE 11

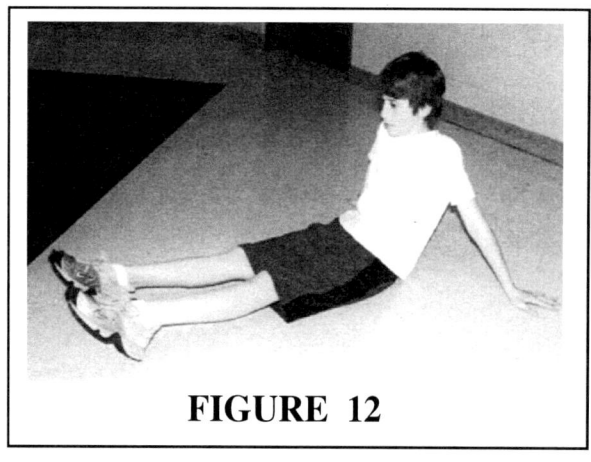

FIGURE 12

Exercise No. 10- Ankle Stretch

This stretching exercise is for ankle area muscles and tendons. From the sitting position, have them put both feet, with relaxed toes up, out in front of them with feet together. Arms out at their sides for balance. Next keeping the legs flat to the floor or ground, have them roll both ankles forward pushing the toes down. Hold that position for 3 seconds, then relax the feet back to the starting position. Next, keeping the heels flat to the floor, have them roll both ankles back towards their head with the toes pointing up. This should be a hard pull, with the toes, hard towards their head. Hold that position 3 seconds, then relax the feet back to the starting position. Repeat this at least 5 times in both positions *(SEE FIGURE 12)*.

Exercise No. 11- Wrist Stretch

This stretching exercise is for the wrist area muscles and tendons. From the standing position, have them put both feet about shoulder width apart. Then have them put both arms straight out to their sides. Next, with their fingers spread slightly apart and pointing straight out, have them roll both hands at the wrist joint, with the fingers spread to as far down as they can. Hold that position for several seconds, then relax the hands back to the starting position. Next, from the starting position, have them roll both hands up as far as they can at the wrist joint, with the fingers spread. Hold that position for 3 seconds, then relax the hands back to the starting position. Repeat this at least 5 times, in both positions *(SEE FIGURE 13)*.

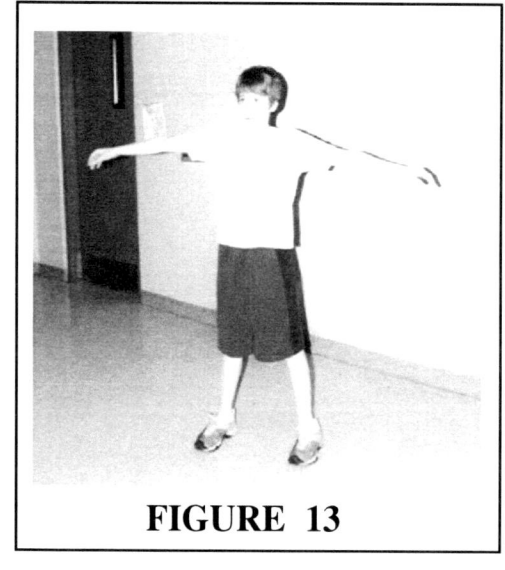

FIGURE 13

Exercise No. 12- Neck Stretch

This stretching exercise is for the neck muscles. From the standing position, have them put their hands down at their sides, turn to the right and put their chin on the right shoulder. Hold for 3 seconds, then relax. Next move the head back to center, and put the chin on their chest. Hold that position for 3 seconds, and relax. Then turn to the left, and put their chin on the left shoulder. Hold that position for 3 seconds,

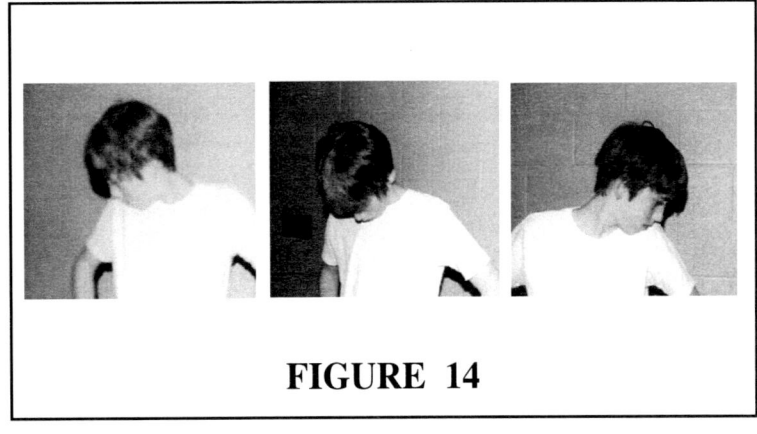

FIGURE 14

then relax. Repeat this at least 5 times, for all 3 of the positions *(SEE FIGURE 14)*.

Drills for Coordination and Agility

These drills are designed to teach him or her how to move around on their feet better, without falling down. These drills will also help them improve their balance and agility. If you son or daughter will do these drills every day, even for a short while, you will notice their coordination improving after just a few weeks.

Drill No. 1 Crossover Foot

The Basics are:
This is called the crossover foot, and side to side, exercise drill. The feet have to keep crossing over each other, from in front to behind. Its an old football drill, but it works great for coordination and agility training. All position players need to work on this drill.

Practice:
Take your son or daughter out to the park, or in your back yard where there is grass and lots of room. They will need grass and lots of room because they will be moving side to side for about 40 or 50 yards, the grass will help cushion them if they fall. And they usually do that a lot at first. Stand in front of them and face each other at about three yards apart. You do the same steps they do,` and both of you need to be moving in the same direction. Start out with

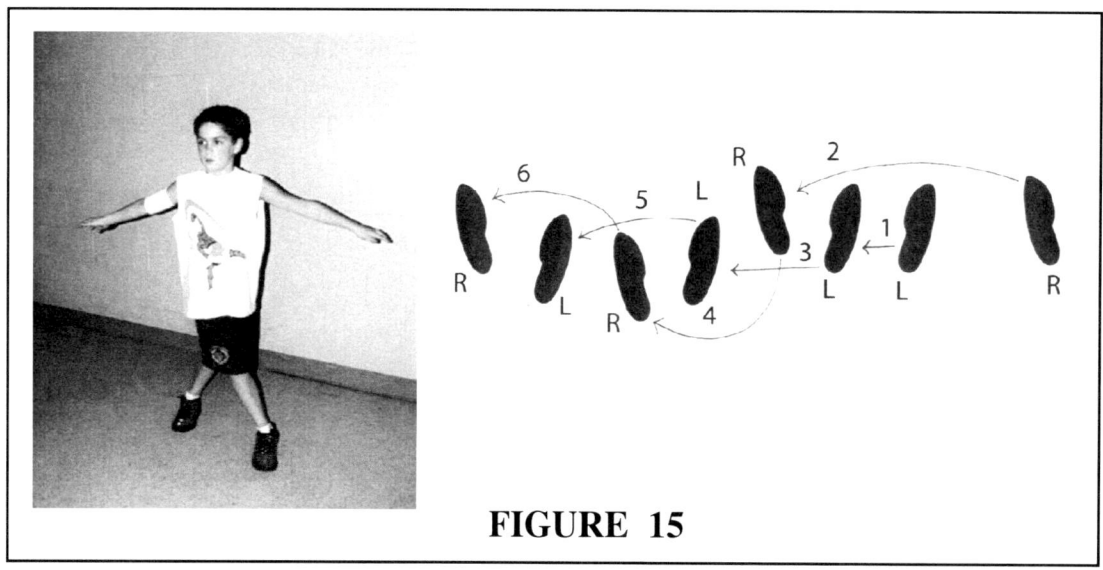

FIGURE 15

both of you walking through this slowly until you can learn how to move your feet. Then speed up little by little until you both get better at it. Start with the feet apart, then have them step to their left with their left foot.

Next step to the left, with their right foot crossing over the top of their left foot. Then step again to the left, with their left foot crossing behind their right foot. Next step again to the left, with the right foot crossing behind their left foot. Then step again to the left, with the left foot over the top of the right foot. Then keep repeating this combination of steps to the left, over and over, for about 30 yards. Then stop and reverse these steps, going to their right, first with their left foot over their right foot, and so on, for about 30 yards to the right. Keeping their hands straight out to their sides will help them keep their balance. The better they get at doing this, you can speed the process up little by little. After a few weeks your son or daughter should be able to do this drill on the run, and without falling down. If not, keep working with them and don't give up because they can learn to do it. *(SEE FIGURE15).*

Drill No. 2- Running Backwards

The Basics are:

This is called the running backwards exercise drill. It is running backwards, with the feet and arm pumping up and down. What this drill will do is, help them when they need to back peddle down the court. All position players need to work on this drill.

Practice:

You will need to find a very large back yard, or a big area in a park with thick grass. The reason I am suggesting thick grass is, it will help cushion their fall a little if they fall backwards. You will have to go slow at first because there is a danger of falling backwards, and getting whip lash to the neck and head. First both you and your son or daughter line up side by side about 3 or 4 yards apart, with about 50 yards of clear space behind you. Then both of you start slowly jogging backwards while pumping your arms up and down. Do this for about 50 yards, then stop and repeat the drill for about 50 yards back to where you started. Usually one or both of you will fall down the first few times you try this drill. If either of you fall down, laugh and

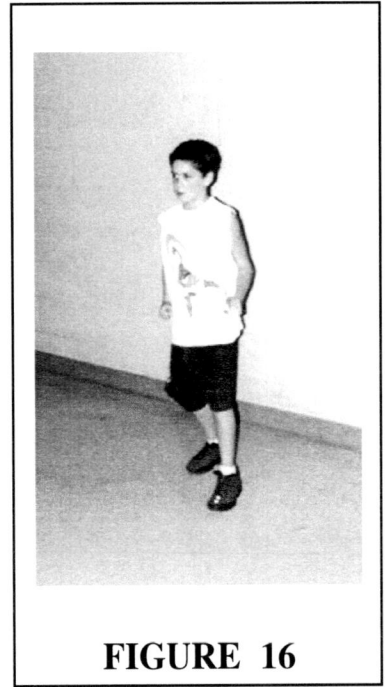

FIGURE 16

make a joke out of it. If you criticize them too much, they may not want to do it any more. If your son or daughter is falling down, and you are not, then you may want to fall down a few times yourself. This is so they will think that it is hard for you also, and they won't get discouraged. This usually works in keeping them interested. Also shout encouragement to them as you are running side by side. The secret for keeping your balance is, raising your knees up high while pumping your hands up and down as fast as you can. Once they can run fast for about 50 yards, and not fall down, you will notice their interest level go up. When they do become good at this, then you can change the drill a little to make it harder. A suggestion on how to do this might be, have them run backwards about 10 or 15 yards. Then blow a whistle, have them turn around without stopping, and run forward in the same direction. Keep doing this, and change directions, at a full run about every 10 or 15 yards. This drill alone is one of the best drills for kids that I have ever seen, that will really improve on their coordination and agility *(SEE FIGURE 16)*.

Drills for Strength

These drills are designed to build up your son or daughters strength. They are not to build them into a muscle bound weight lifter, just enough to tone up their muscles so they will be a little more stronger. Many young kids these days just sit around home a lot and don't have a lot of chores to do as they did years ago, possibly on a farm. And because they have very little to do with their arms, like pitch hay or carry buckets of milk, the arms and legs are weak. It is important that your son or daughter do some of these drills every day. If they get tired and quit for a week or two, the drills will not help them very much. Make sure to follow all breathing instructions on each drill because they are very important.

Because there are different parts of the body that need strengthening, we will break this down into the upper back, lower back, chest, shoulders, arms, abdominal, legs, and how they will help the different playing positions. For a good weight training program, a utility bench and a lightweight barbell set for kids would be great if you can afford it. If not, at least get a dumbbell set. They should start with 3.3 or 4 pound dumbbells, at 5 years old, and work up to 6.6 or 7 pound dumbbells.

UPPER BACK

Drill No. 3- Dumbbell Rowing

The Basics are:

This drill is good for guards and small forwards, for shooting fallaway jumpers. And for centers and power forwards, to give them strength to pull rebounds away from opponents. It is pulling the hands up and down, with a dumbbell.

FIGURE 17

Practice:

Have them hold a dumbbell in their left hand, with the palm facing in, and to the left of a utility bench, table, or couch. Then have them put their right hand on the top of the bench, table, or couch, for support. Next they should bend forward at the hips until their back is parallel to the floor and arched, with the knees bent slightly. Their left arm should hang down. Then while in this position, they pull the left arm up until the elbow is pointing toward the ceiling. Then they lower the dumbbell slowly back down. They should feel a slight pull along the right outside of their back. This is working the Latissimus

Dorsi muscles (Lats) along the back. Then have them turn around, switch to the right hand, and repeat this process. Have them take a deep breath just before they start to pull up, and let it out slowly as they are letting the dumbbell back down. For the 5 year olds, they should do about 5 of these with each arm. As they get a little older and stronger, they can increase this number and go to the heavier dumbbells *(SEE FIGURE 17)*.

LOWER BACK

Drill No. 4- Straight Leg Deadlift

The Basics are:

It is lifting up dumbbell's, from the floor, by straightening up the legs. They need the strength when they get screened out by bigger stronger forwards, and centers. This drill is good for all players, but mostly for guards, and maybe small forwards, in helping them to move quickly out on the perimeter while playing defense.

Practice:

Have them stand straight up with a dumbbell in each hand and with their palms facing their stomach. Their knees should be slightly bent, with the legs about shoulder width apart. Next they should lower the dumbbells by bending over, using their back not their arms. They should keep the dumbbells close to their shins, and their head should be up. While they are doing this their hips should be moving backwards. Have them take a deep breath just as they start to bend down, and let it out slowly as they come back up. For 5 year olds start out with about 5 of these, then increase the number later as they get stronger and older *(SEE FIGURE 18)*.

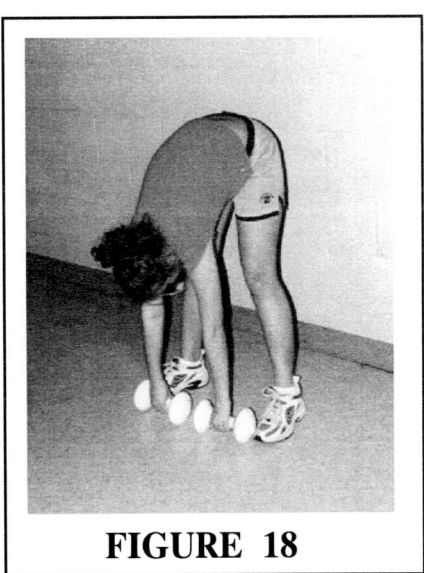

FIGURE 18

Drill No. 5- Back Extension

The Basics are:

This is laying down, extending both the hands and the legs, then raising the feet and the hands up slightly off the floor. This drill is good for

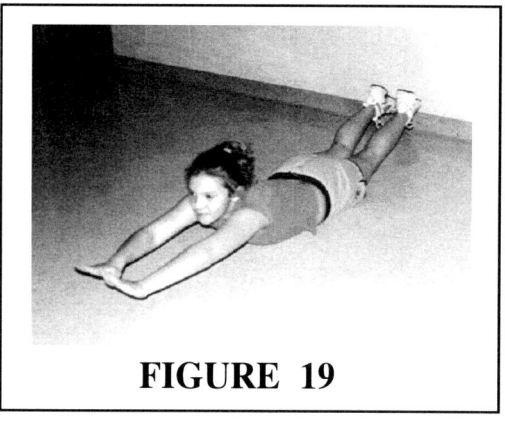

FIGURE 19

guards and small forwards for the same reasons as above in drill No.4.

Practice:

Have them lay down on their stomach on a floor or flat surface, with both arms straight out in front of them. They should face their palms down, and their legs straight out behind them. Next they should pull in their abdominal muscles, like they would be creating a small space between their stomach and the floor. Then have them lift both arms and legs, just a few inches up off the floor. They need to hold that position for about 5 seconds. While doing this, they need to stretch out in front and in back as much as they can. Then lower the arms and legs slowly. Have them take a deep breath just as they lift the arms and legs, then let it out slowly as they lower them. They should start out doing about 5 of these, and increase it a little as they get stronger *(SEE FIGURE 19)*.

CHEST

Drill No. 6- Chest Press

The Basics are:

This is pressing, or pushing, up dumbbell's in each hand. This helps players build up their upper body strength. This drill is good for centers, and power forwards, to help give them pushing, and holding position, strength under the basket.

Practice:

Have them lay down on a utility bench, with a dumbbell in each hand, and with their feet on the floor. Then have them push both of their arms up directly over their shoulders, with their palms facing forward. Next have them bring the dumbbells back down slowly to their sides, with the elbow just a little lower

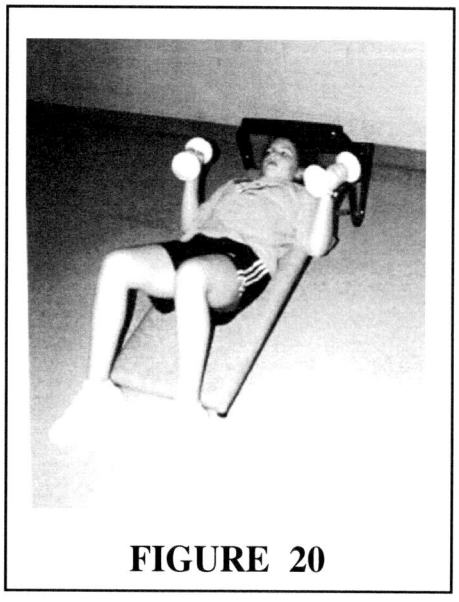

FIGURE 20

than their shoulders. Then have them push the dumbbells back up again. While doing this they should pull in the stomach abdominals, but don't push their back into the flat surface. All during this their shoulder blades should not raise up off the bench. Start out with 5 year olds doing about 5 of these, up through 12 year olds doing about 10. Have them take a deep breath, just before they push the dumbbells up, and let it out slowly as they bring them back down. For the 9 to 12 year olds if you don't have a barbell set, you can substitute dumbbells for the barbell weight. I don't advise the barbells, for the real little kids because it might be to much for them to handle. They can use them when they are a little bit older. And they can do a few more repetitions also once they get a little bit older and stronger *(SEE FIGURE 20)*.

SHOULDERS

Drill No. 7- The Shoulder Shrug

The Basics are:
This is lifting up dumbbell's in each hand, from a hanging down position, up to the shoulders position. This helps players build up their upper body strength. The drill is good for centers, and power forwards, to give them lifting strength under the basket.

Practice:
Have them stand straight up, with their feet about shoulder width apart, and with a dumbbell in each hand. Their arms should hang straight down, turned with the palms facing the stomach in front of their thighs. Have them tuck in their chin towards their chest, and pull in their abdominal muscles. Their knees should be relaxed. Next have them shrug their shoulder up towards their ears, then slowly lower their shoulders back down to the arms hanging position. Have them take a deep breath, just before they shrug up their shoulders, then let it back out slowly as they lower their shoulders. Start out with the 5 year olds doing about 5 of these, up through the 12 year olds doing 10 of these. They

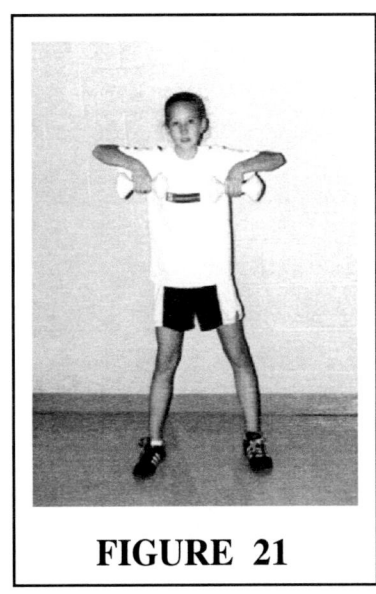

FIGURE 21

FIGURE 22

can do a few more of these once they get a little older and stronger *(SEE FIGURE 21)*.

Drill No. 8- Shoulder front Raise

The Basics are:

This is lifting up dumbbell's in each hand, from a hanging down position, to a straight out from the shoulders position. This drill is good for same reasons as the above drill number 7, and it should make dribbling easier on the arms

Practice:

Have them stand straight up, with their feet about shoulder width apart, and with a dumbbell in each hand. Their arms should hang straight down, turned with the palms facing the stomach in front of their thighs. Then they should pull in their abdominal muscles, and have their knees relaxed. Next have them raise their right arm straight out in front of them, to about shoulder height, and then slowly lower it back down to the arms hanging position. They should take a deep breath, just before they raise their arm, and let it out slowly as they lower their arm. Next they should repeat the process with their left arm. Start out with 5 year olds doing about 5 of these with each arm, up through 12 year olds doing about 8 with each arm. They can do a few more of these once they get a little older and stronger *(SEE FIGURE 22)*.

ARMS

Drill No. 9- Wrist Curl

The Basics are:

This is lifting up a dumbbell, from the down position, to the up position. This drill is good for all players, to give them the strength to make long passes. Also this is good for guards or small forwards, to give them strength to make shots way out on the perimeter.

Practice:

Lifting weight should not hurt your son or daughter if you don't over do it with too much weight. This drill should improve their wrist strength, for throwing the long passes. Start with 5 year olds using two 3.3 or 4 pound dumbbells, and then work up to 6.6 or 7 pound dumbbells as they get stronger and older. Its not so much the amount of the weight, but that your son or daughter is working their muscles and tendons. This drill can be done inside or outside of the house. Start by having them sit on the edge of a utility bench, chair, or couch. Next have them spread their legs apart, then take the dumbbell in their right hand. Then have them put their right elbow on the top of the right knee. Next they will take their left hand, and use it to hold down their right hand at the wrist. To start they should have their right palm facing up, then curl it down towards the floor and back up again. 5 year olds should do this about 6 times with the right arm, then switch to the left arm reversing the positions, for about 6 times. 12 year olds should start out doing about 10 of these with each arm. As they get stronger, you can increase the number of repetitions with each arm. Caution here, do not over do it with too many repetitions, and hurt their arm. If they are not strong enough at first, then reduce the number of repetitions on each arm. To judge how strong they are at first, make this observation, they should be just barely able to do the last curl lift, on each set, for each arm. And last have them take a deep breath and hold it just before they start on the down motion, and then letting it out slowly on the upward curl *(SEE FIGURE 23)*.

FIGURE 23

Drill No. 10- Biceps Curl

The Basics are:

This is lifting up a dumbbell, from the down position, to the up position. This drill is good for the same reasons as the previous drill number 9.

Practice:

Have them stand straight up, with their feet about shoulder width apart, and with a dumbbell in each hand. Then have them let their arms hang down at their thighs, with their palms facing out. Next they pull in their abdominal muscles,

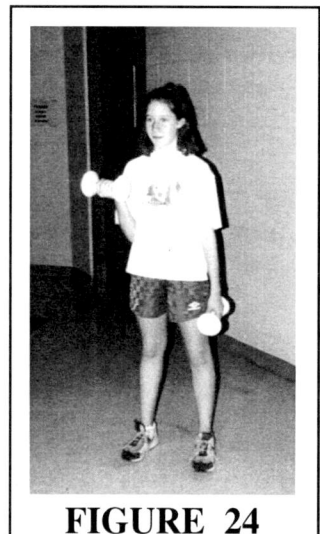

FIGURE 24

and stand up straight, with their knees slightly relaxed. Start by having them curl up their right arm to their shoulder, with the palm facing in towards their shoulder at the top of the movement. Next they slowly lower the arm back down to the starting position. Then they repeat the same process with their left arm. 5 year olds should do about 4 of these with each arm if they can, with 12 year olds doing about 8 with each arm. If 10 to 12 year olds have a light weight barbell set, they can substitute it to do their curls. A word of caution here, don't put to much weight on the barbell to where they can't do at least 8 curls They can do a few more when they get a little older or stronger. Have them take a deep breath, just before they start to curl up the dumbbell or barbell, and let it out slowly as they start on the downward motion to lower the arm *(SEE FIGURE 24)*.

ABDOMINALS

Drill No. 11- Sit Up Crunches

The Basics are:

This is just partially sitting up , from a lying down on the back position. This drill is good for all players, to help them reach out farther. It will help them to reach out and grab for balls, and it will help them play defense, to reach out to knock down passes.

Practice:

Have them lay down on the floor on their back, with both knees bent up about 10 to 12 inches high, with feet flat on the floor. They should then fold both hands together across their chest. Next have them raise up just enough to get their neck, and the top of their shoulders, off the floor a little bit. Hold it there for a 5 seconds, then slowly lower back down to the lying position. Each time, just before the raise up, have them take a deep breath and hold it while they raise up. Then have them let it out slowly as they come back down into the lying position. For 5 year olds they should do about 7 of these, with 12 year olds doing about 15. If they can't do this many, then have them do as many as they can without struggling. Then increase the number a little bit as they get stronger or older *(SEE FIGURE 25)*.

Drill No. 12- Abdominal Slide

The Basics are:
This is sliding both feet up, keeping heels against the floor, from the fully extended legs position. This drill is good for the same reasons as the previous drill number 11.

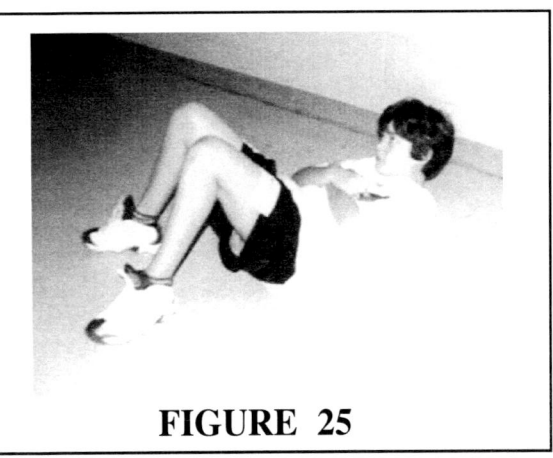

FIGURE 25

Practice:
Have them lay down on the floor on their back, with legs about shoulder width apart, and knees bent up about 10 to 12 inches high. Their toes should point up, and they should dig their heels into the floor, with their shoes off. Their arms should be at their sides. Next have them pull in their abdominal muscles, and lightly push the small of their back into the floor, so it is flat against it. Then have them slowly slide their heels forward while still digging their heels into the floor, towards fully extending their legs and holding the rest of this position. They must keep their abdominal muscles pulled in, and keep their back flat against the floor while sliding their legs down towards the flat on the floor position. This may be hard for them to do at first, so have them continue to pull in the abdominals, then hold the back flat to the floor for as long as they can as they try to straighten their legs. For 5 year olds have them start out by doing at least 3 of these, with 12 year olds doing 6. Or do as many as they can until they get stronger. Have them take a deep breath, just before they start the slide, and let it out very slowly as they slide the legs down to the fully extended position *(SEE FIGURE 26)*.

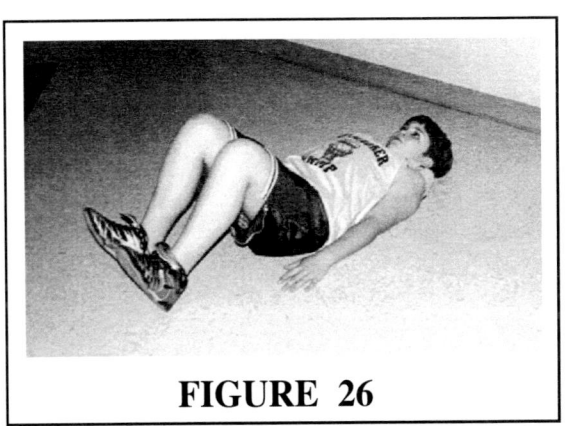

FIGURE 26

LEGS, TOES, ANKLES

Drill No. 13- Toe Raise

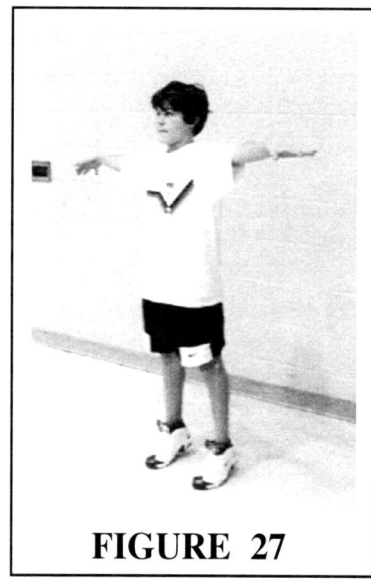

FIGURE 27

The Basics are:
This is raising way up on the toes and holding, to strengthen the lower legs, toes, and ankles. This drill is good for all the players because they need to be able to jump up as high as possible. Centers, and power forwards, really need to work on these because they have to push off, and jump straight up more often for rebounds. It will help them improve their jump shots, and rebounding abilities also.

Practice:
Have them stand up straight, with their feet about shoulder width, and arms out at their sides for balance. Then they raise up on their toes as high as they can go. Have them hold that position for 5 seconds. Then they come slowly back down to the starting position. 5 year olds should start out trying to do about 3 of these, with 12 year olds doing about 6. They can increase the number of repetitions, by a few as they get stronger. Have them take a deep breath, just before they start to push up, and let it out slowly as they come back down to the standing position *(SEE FIGURE 27)*.

THIGHS

Drill No. 14- Wall Sits

The Basics are:
This is another exercise is to strengthen the quadriceps (front thigh), hamstrings, gluteal (buttocks), and back muscles. This exercise helps all players train their muscles, for the "ready" stance as well as their jumping ability.

Practice:
Have your son or daughter stand next to a wall, then put both feet together about 1-1/2 feet out in front of them. Next they put both hands up, and out to their sides, palms up, then their back slides down the wall until their thighs are

parallel to the floor. They should take a deep breath before they slide down the wall, then hold the down position for at least 10 seconds. Also let me point out here that they should slide down the wall far enough, to feel a tightening in their front and back thigh muscles. Then as they straighten back up to the starting position, they slowly expel the air, then thgey relax for half a minute or so. Have them start out by doing about 3 or 5 of these. If they are a large boy or girl, still carrying a lot of baby fat, they may not be able to do that many. In that case start them out with the most they can easily do, without struggling too much, and increase the numbers as they get stronger *(SEE FIGURE 28)*.

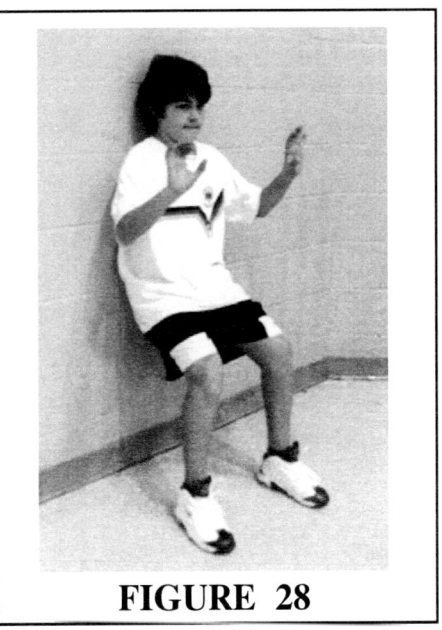

FIGURE 28

Drills for Running

Drill No. 15- Wind Sprint Ladders Running

The Basics are:

This is running out to a set distance, touching down, and going back to the starting point. Then touching down at the starting point, and running out to a longer distance, touching down, and running back to the starting point. The distance they run out keeps increasing as they touch the starting point. This drill is good for all players to build up speed, endurance, and strong muscles in their legs. Since basketball players are running almost all the time, they all need to work on this drill to keep themselves in shape. This drill is designed to increase their speed, but it will also help their agility a little bit.

Practice:

If you don't have a football field close by, with white yard line markers, this will take a little work to set up. Beware, before they even start this drill, have them jog around for 5 to 10 minutes to get their muscles properly warmed up. Next, since this is an explosive type drill, have them do at least 8 to 10 hamstring stretches to keep them from getting hurt. To make the yard line markers, try using old white plastic milk bottles filled with sand, kitty litter, or water, to weight it down. You can take a wide tip black felt permanent marker, and mark 0, 10, 20, 30, 40, on them in great big letters. They make great yard markers, and you are recycling for the environment. Next estimate, or measure out a 40 yard distance. Put one bottle, marked "0", down at the starting point. Then go down about 40 yards, and put another one down marked "40". Now in your mind divide the distance between the two bottles into 4 equal spaces, of 10 yards long. Then go out from the start 10 yards, put down the bottle marked "10", then out another 10 yards and put down the bottle marked "20", then 10 more yards and the bottle marked 30. Now you have a 40 yard course set out. Here is how the ladders work. Have your son or daughter go to the starting point. On the command "GO", have them charge out straight ahead at full speed for 10 yards, then they are to stop quickly and touch either hand down on the ground, turn and run back to the starting line. They will know when they have gone 10 yards, by looking over at the milk bottle. And always looking over at the milk bottles will tell them when to touch down. Now, at the starting point, they stop again, quickly touch either hand down, then they turn and run out to the 20 yard marker. Again they touch down, then turn and run back to the starting point. Then they touch down again, turn, and run out to the 30 yard marker. Then they touch down again, turn, and run back to the starting point. In other words they will be increasing the distance they run, by 10 yards, each time they touch down at the starting point. The last time they will be running the whole 40 yards, then touching down, and running back the 40 yards to the starting point. Have them try to do at least one set of these, every time you practice this drill. Later on if they can do more than one set, and they are not too tired, its ok *(SEE FIGURE 29)*.

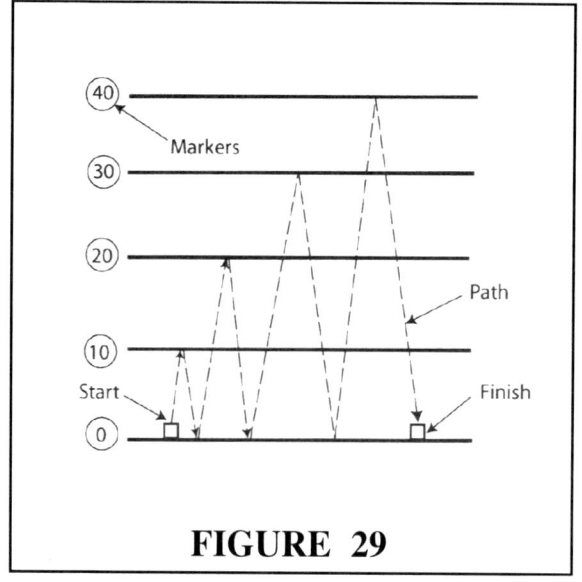

FIGURE 29

Drill No. 16- Speed Burst Running

The Basics are:

This is explode out running to a set distance, stopping and walking back to the marker. Resting for a few seconds, then explode out running back to the starting point. Next resting at the starting point for a few seconds, then explode running out to the next longer distance. Then resting again, and explode running back to the starting point. The distance they run out keeps increasing as they explode run out from the starting point. This drill is for all players, to improve on their quickness. After they have been doing this drill for awhile, you can speed up the drill and further improve on their quickness. The beauty of this is when they get on their first team, and you see how fast they are when compared to the other kids their own age, both of you will feel good about having worked with them on this.

Practice:

This is a special quickness running drill. It is called speed bursts. It is a drill that is somewhat like ladders *(SEE FIGURE 29)*. There are several variations, but I like this one best for young boys or girls. I have always ended up coaching the littlest kids, so that's why I am recommending this drill, and because I know it works. Beware before they ever start this drill have them jog around the yard or park a few times, to get their muscles warmed up properly. Next have them do at least 8 or 10 hamstring stretches. This is to keep them from possibly getting hurt. Start off by marking a 20 yard coarse similar to the one in Drill No. 15 *(SEE FIGURE 29)*, except put the yard markers at 5 yard intervals instead of 10 yards apart. When you have the course marked, have your son or daughter go to the starting point of yard "0". On the command "GO", have them explode out from the starting line. Then they run as fast as they can for 5 yards while pumping their knees, and hands, up and down as high as they can. Then at the 5 yard marker, have them stop and catch their breath, turn, and walk back to the 5 yard marker. Next give them a minute to rest, then say "GO", and have them run as fast as they can back to the "0" yard marker. Then they turn, and walk back to the "0" yard marker while catching their breath. Then let them stand there at the "0" yard marker, and rest a minute. Then say "Go", and have them run out to the 10 yard marker the same way and stop, then turn, and come back to the 10 yard marker. Then they rest a minutes, then say "GO", and they run back to the "0" yard marker. They keep doing this until they get all the way out to the 20 yard marker, going 5 yards more each time. Make sure they pump their hands up and down, and get their knees up as high as they can.

If they get too tired, stop the drill until they can build up their stamina, to get all the way through one complete set. This drill will be very tough, on boys or girls that are big for their age, or overweight, so be patient and keep encouraging them. If they are having trouble, then try going just a little bit farther each day or week as you see that their endurance is building up. One time through the whole

20 yards once a day, should be more than enough for a 5 year old. That would be a big accomplishment, for even the best of 5 year olds.

Drills for Passing the Basketball

Passing the basketball is a very important phase of the basketball game. As many of the great coaches have said, "The quickest kid on the team can not outrun the ball". To get the ball up court quickly, or to get the ball to the open person, is what offensive basketball is about. On defense its about intercepting a pass, then passing it quickly to your team mate breaking to your basket at the opposite end of the court. Passes are probably the most effective way to attack a defense, and get the ball up court. Before you start any passing drills with your son or daughter, you might try this little demonstration. Tell them that anyone that can run from the baseline to mid court before you throw the ball to mid court, or from the garage out to the sidewalk, will get a free Hamburger, coke, and fries. To make it even more interesting, give them a three step head start before you throw the ball. Explain to them that this is why passing, to move the ball up court, is quicker than dribbling it up court. When ever they make a good pass make sure to make a big deal out of it, just like you would if they shoot a basket and score. Any player on the team, who can find the open person to get the ball to, is a very valuable player to the team. Impress on your son or daughter that when they make a good pass, they make it easier for their team mates to shoot the ball, and it demoralizes the opponents defense. If you don't get home from work until late in the day, your son or daughter can practice after school by finding a wall and using it to get the ball back to them. This way they can get their practice in every day while its light outside.

Drill No. 17- Both Hands Chest Pass

The Basics are:

This is push passing the ball in the air, using both hands. This drill is mostly for guards, and small forwards, but centers, and power forwards, also have to pass even though it's not as often. So, whatever position your son or daughter plays, make sure to work at least a little bit each day with them on their passing skills. The basics for making a two handed pass are, have them grab the basketball with both hands and hold it at their chest level *(SEE FIGURE 30, STEP 1)*. Their thumbs should be facing in towards each other, just as they start the pass.

As they are pushing out with the pass, their hands should be twisting to the outsides, with palms facing outward away from each other, thumbs down, just as they release the ball *(SEE FIGURE 30, STEP 2)*. Also they need to step out with the left foot if they are right handed, and the right foot if they are left handed *(SEE FIGURE 30)*. The stepping out helps them get more speed and power on the pass.

STEP 2   STEP 1
FIGURE 30

Practice:

To practice this technique, start out with your son or daughter passing every day for about 5 to 10 minutes, no matter what position they play. Especially the younger 5 through 8 year olds need to work on this. Go out to your driveway, or back yard, and go out about 5 yards away from your son or daughter. Next have them push pass the ball toward you in the air. Once they begin to get more proficient at making this pass, you may want to vary the drill. Have them stay stationary, and you move from side to side, so they can learn how to hit a moving target. Make sure they aim, and pass it directly at your chest area, and make sure their fingers are in the right position. For 12 year olds, you might want to move out about 7 or 8 yards away from them for this drill.

Drill No. 18- Both Hands Bounce Pass

The Basics are:

This is push bounce passing the ball on the ground, using both hands. This drill is for the same reasons, and the same players as mentioned in drill number 17. But it is more difficult to intercept because the defender has to reach down closer to the floor. The basics for making the two handed bounce pass are, have them hold the ball in the same grip, and location as in the chest pass *(SEE FIGURE 31, STEP 1)*. Except they push the ball hard, down against the floor or driveway. Starting out the pass is the same as the chest pass, however just as they release the ball, they rotate the palms outward, with their thumbs down.

STEP 2　　　**STEP 1**
FIGURE 31

The hands should be facing outward, and slightly pointed downward on the follow through *(SEE FIGURE 31, STEP 2)*. Also they need to learn how to aim the ball so that it hits the floor, or driveway, about three fourths of the way toward you. And it has to bounces back up into the receivers hands on one bounce. Also they need to step out with the left foot if they are right handed, and the right foot if they are left handed *(SEE FIGURE 31)*. The stepping out helps them get more speed and power on the pass.

Practice:

To practice this technique, start out with your son or daughter passing every day for about 5 to 10 minutes, no matter what position they play. Especially the younger 5 through 8 year olds need to work on this. Next you, mom or dad, move out to about the same distances as in the chest pass. Stand still at first until they get better at making this pass, then move from side to side so they get practice at hitting a moving target. When you are moving, you will have to explain to them that the pass should be aimed just a little in front of you so that you don't have to stop, and reach back to get it. Also the pass should bounce up so that it gets to you at about chest high. This way you can control the ball better than if it bounces way over your head, or way down at your feet. Check and make sure they aim and pass so that it gets to you directly at your chest area, and make sure their fingers are in the right position in the follow through.

Drill No. 19- Both Hands Overhead Pass

The Basics are:

This is push passing the ball in the air, using both hands. This drill is for the same reasons as in drill number 17, 18. However, since centers and power forwards have to make long passes more often than the other players, they may need to work more on this type of pass. However, this pass is hard to throw with a lot of accuracy. For the little kids, you may not want to work on this pass as much as the other types of passes because sometimes it's a very hard pass to complete. If they have ever played any soccer though this will be easy, and familiar, for them to do.

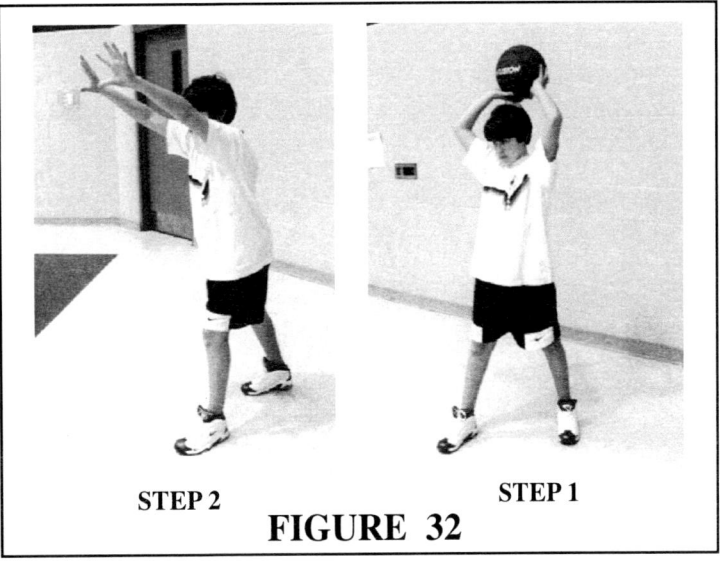

STEP 2   STEP 1
FIGURE 32

The basics for making the two handed overhead pass are, first have them grab the ball the same way as described in drill 17, except hold it up about head high *(SEE FIGURE 32, STEP 1)*. Then as they push and release the ball, out toward their target, they need to rotate the hands outward, thumbs down, and snap their wrists *(SEE FIGURE 32, STEP 2)*. If you don't snap your wrists the ball tends to sail high, and over the head of the person you want to get it to. Also they need to step way out with the foot opposite the strong hand, to get more momentum and distance on the pass *(SEE FIGURE 32, STEP 2)*.

Practice:

To practice this pass go out to the driveway and get up by the garage door. Then have your son or daughter go out by the sidewalk side of the drive way, and make a long pass up to you. Or go out to the back yard, and get about 5 yards away from each other. They should aim the ball high enough, to get it to you at about chest high. If your 5 year old can't get the ball out that far then move in closer, just enough, so they can reach you with the pass. Also make sure they step out with the right foot if they are right handed, and the left foot if they are left handed *(SEE FIGURE 31)*. Again, the stepping out helps them get more speed and power on the pass. All players should know how to make this pass even though they may not use it that often.

Drill No. 20- One Handed Pass

The Basics are:

This is over the head snap passing the ball in the air, using both hands.

FIGURE 33 — STEP 2, STEP 1

This drill is mostly for guards and small forwards, but centers, and power forwards, also have to pass even though it's not as often. So, whatever position your son or daughter plays, make sure to work at least a little bit with them, on this passing skill.

The basics for making a one handed pass are, start out by grabbing it with both hands *(SEE FIGURE 33, STEP 1)*. This is a must for little kids because their hands are so small. The weak hand supports the ball, and the strong hand is right behind the ball *(SEE FIGURE 34)*. When you are ready to pass the ball, you step right at the player the pass is going to, using the left foot. Then you push it with your right hand, aiming the ball so it gets to the player about chest high *(SEE FIGURE 33, STEP 2)*. One handed passes can be in the air, or bounced to a team mate. On the follow through the ball should roll off the finger tips.

Practice:

To practice this pass go out to the driveway, and get up by the garage door. Then have your son or daughter go out by the sidewalk side of the drive way, and make a pass up to you. Or go out to the back yard, and get about 5 yards away from each other. They should aim the ball to get it to you at about chest high. If your 5 year old can't get the ball out that far then move in closer, just enough, so they can reach you with the pass. Also make sure they step out with the left foot if they are right handed, and the right foot if they are left handed *(SEE FIGURE 33, STEP 2)*. Again, the stepping out helps them get more speed and power on the pass. It is a good idea to teach them to make this pass with either hand. This is be-

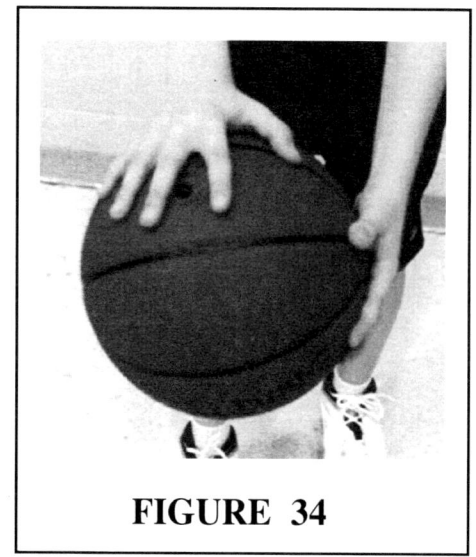

FIGURE 34

cause it's a good type of pass to use when you want to get the ball around an opponent, standing in front of you.

Drills for Dribbling the Basketball

Dribbling the basketball is another very important part of the game of basketball. As a parent you should start teaching them how to dribble as soon as they are 5 years old. It is the number one skill to learn in basketball, and probably the hardest for some boys and girls to learn. One good thing is, it won't cost too much to get them started, just a basketball and a hard surface is needed. It is a coordination skill, and if they keep working at it they can learn how to do it. Probably the first thing to explain to them about dribbling is, have them learn right from the start, to **use their fingertips and not the palm of the hand.** The fingertips is where the control comes from. And mom or dad here is a tip for you, the more they dribble the better they will get, and the better they get the more confidence they will have. Another tip, if you want to see how good they are doing when you come home later, and they have been out practicing, then check their hands. The fingertips should be dirty and the palms clean.

They should learn also to **keep the bouncing ball close to them**. If you watch the good dribblers, the ball will be like a Yo-Yo on a string as they move around with it. The best way to start out practicing with them is, have them just stand still and get used to dribbling right in front of themselves, using the fingers. You need to supervise them closely at first, to make sure they are learning the concept correctly. Next you can have them walk slowly while dribbling. When they learn to do that correctly, then they can run while dribbling. If it appears they will always be small in size, then keep working on this with them over and over. Some of the best dribblers and ball handlers ever, took the ball with them everywhere they went and just kept dribbling, and dribbling, and dribbling.

Drill No. 20- The Basic Dribble

The Basics are:

Dribbling is when a player uses one hand to bounce the basketball continuously, without interruption. The dribble ends when this action is interrupted, such as holding the ball when it comes up to the players hand. It ends by grabbing it with both hands, or placing the hand at the side, on the lower half of the ball, or underneath, then rotating the hand before pushing the

FIGURE 35

ball down, and starting to dribble again. In other words if you do not redirect the ball towards the floor after it touches your hand in any way, the dribble has ended. When the dribble has ended, you *can not* hesitate, then start to dribble again. You have to pass the ball to someone else.

The correct stance for learning how to dribble is, start by standing in the upright position and stay in one place. Then if you are right handed, your left foot should staggered out in front of your right foot, with both feet parallel to each other *(SEE FIGURE 35)*. Your knees should be bent slightly, and ball in hand. The upper arm is close to the body, and the lower arm is extended out to the ball. Now you are ready to push the ball down to the floor. If you are left handed, everything is just the opposite, with the right foot out in front of the left. All players should know how to dribble. But mostly "Point Guards", and "Shooting Guards", need to work on their basics when they are starting out.

Practice:

It might be a good idea to make a 2-1/2 foot square, or a circle the same size, for young kids to start out practicing in. Use tape to make this on the basketball court floor, or use cones to mark the area. Then have your son or daughter stand in this area, and get into the correct stance for right, or left, handed dribbling. Next with ball in hand, have them slowly dribble in place. Make sure they stay inside the area. When they are just starting out, it's ok to have them look at where they ar dribbling the ball. Once they demonstrate they can do this correctly, they can move on to the ball handling moves.

Drill No. 21- No Look Dribbling

The Basics are:

Dribbling the basketball without looking at the ball. Teach them, **don't watch the ball as you dribble** *(SEE FIGURE 36)*. When they are first starting out, you will have to really watch them to make sure they don't look. It's learning to feel the ball with your finger tips. I guess you could say, it might be similar to typing, without looking at the keyboard. All players should be able to "no look" dribble. But mostly "Point Guards", and "Shooting Guards", need to work on this drill.

Practice:

A good way to teach them this lesson is you, mom or dad, stand out about 6 or 7 feet in front of them, and hold up anywhere from one to five fingers. And have your hand raised up in the air. Then have them dribble the ball while standing in place. Next as they are dribbling it in front of them, they have to watch you, and see how many fingers you are holding up. To

FIGURE 36

keep telling you how many fingers you are holding up, they have to look up and take their eyes off the ball, in order see your fingers. Then after they have been doing this drill for awhile, have them keep standing still in the same place while continuing to dribble the ball. Then you move around them in a circle, holding up your fingers. They can turn their head to look, but not their feet. Then last of all after they have been doing all of these drills for awhile, have them try to dribble the ball 5 or 6 straight times, and with their eyes closed.

Drill No. 22- Either Hand Dribbling

The Basics are:

Teach them to dribble with either hand. If you start teaching them young, they can learn how to do this. When they can dribble with either hand, it makes them twice as hard to guard. If the person guarding a player notices that you only dribble with the one hand, they could over play you towards the side you are dribbling on. And this could force you way out away from the basket. Bend the knees, stay low to protect the ball *(SEE FIGURE 36),* and don't look at it. All players should be able to dribble with either hand. Even big tall kids can learn how to do this if you start working with them when they are young. But mostly "Point Guards", "Shooting Guards", and "Small Forwards", need to work on this drill.

Practice:

To start out, have them stand in place and dribble about 10 or 15 times with the strong hand. Then switch and dribble about 10 or 15 times with the weak hand. Then when they get better with either hand, have them dribble from the garage out to the sidewalk with the right hand. Then quickly switch and dribble back to the garage with the left hand. A *TIP* here is, have them dribble with their weakest hand when they are out practicing. This will probably be their left hand if they are right handed, and their right hand if they are left handed. Watch them, and make sure they stay low, and see they don't look at the ball.

Drills for Ball Handling

Drill No. 23- Dribbling Techniques

Generally Speaking when dribbling up court:

Stay low and protect the ball when you are in traffic (lots of players around you). The knees are bent a little, and the hand has to stay on top of the ball. The forefinger on the dribbling hand should be pointed straight ahead. When an opponent confronts you, stay in position, and keep your body between the opponent and the ball. There are many moves a player can make while dribbling the ball. They are a fast high speed (upright position) dribble, a slow low speed protective dribble, the hesitate or stutter step dribble, the around the back dribble, the switch hands crossover dribble, the through the legs dribble, the spin move dribble, the shuffle dribble, the stop and go dribble, and the change of pace dribble. All players should know how to basically handle the ball, but especially "Point Guards", and "Shooting Guards", have to work on these drills.

FIGURE 37

Fast High Speed dribble

The Basics are:

Dribbling the ball at high speed, using an explosive move. Like driving around an opponent to the basket for a layup *(SEE FIGURE 37)*. Or dribbling on a fast break from back court, to get the ball up court. Either dribble must be a higher up dribble as compared to the low slow speed dribble. Dribbling low, and bent over, will slow down the speed of the dribble. The ball should come up to about waist high on the dribble. Keep the ball out in front and to the side, so you won't accidentally kick it *(SEE FIGURE 38)*. They should be able to dribble at this high speed with either hand. This is because you might have to come into the basket from either side. Mostly "Point Guards", "Shooting Guards", and "Small Forwards", need to work on this drill.

FIGURE 38

Practice:

To practice this drill, you will will have to find a basketball court, or maybe some corner of a large parking lot. Obviously the basketball court would be better, but it is hard to find one these days that is not being used all the time. Take some cones and set them out to mark an area, about the size of a basketball court, which is 50 feet wide by 84 feet long.

To practice the high speed down the court dribble, have them dribble all the way up one side of the court with the right hand, then around and down the other side with the left hand *(SEE FIGURE 39)*. First have them dribble slowly, almost walking up and down. Then when they master the technique, have them speed it up little by little. The ball should always be dribbled, on the outside of the court side. This is to keep your body between the opponent and the ball.

To practice the high speed explosive dribble to the basket, have them go out to the right side of the half court line *(SEE FIGURE 40)*. If you don't have a court, you will have to go way out by the sidewalk, and start from there. Or if you don't have a half court line, measure out a distance of about 40 feet from the basket, to start. Then say "GO", and have them fire out using a high speed right handed dribble, and go right to the basket for a layup shot. Make sure the

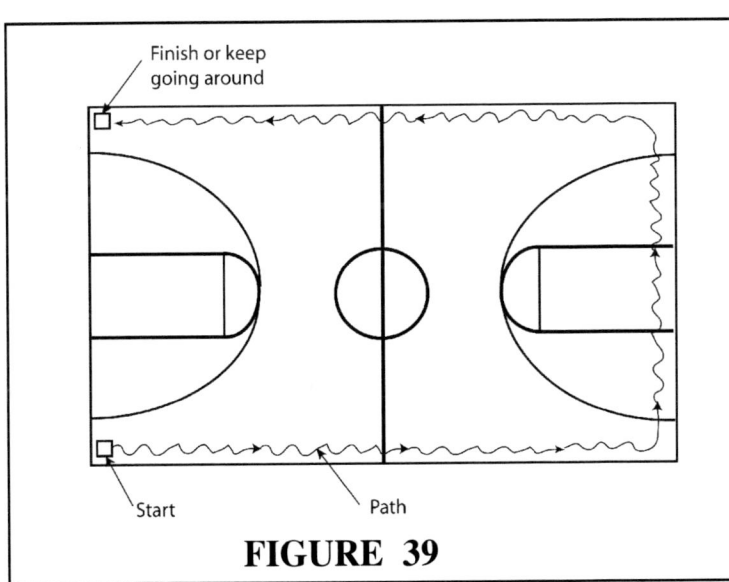

FIGURE 39

49

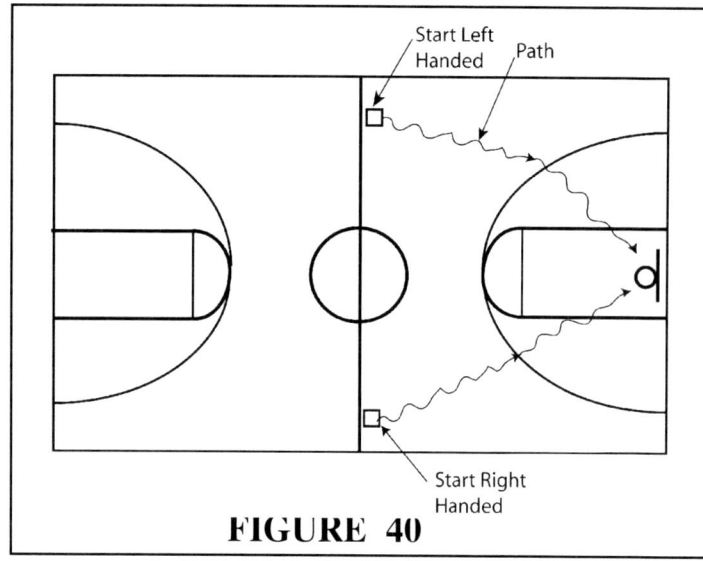
FIGURE 40

really explode out, at high speed, right from the start. Also make sure the dribble is up to waist high, and they are upright with the head up *(SEE FIGURE 37)*, all the way to the basket until they make their jump. Next have them go over to the left side of the half court line, and explode dribble to the basket with the left hand.

Slow Low Speed Dribble

The Basics are:

Dribbling the ball at a low speed, keeping low, and protecting the ball *(SEE FIGURE 36)*. The knees have to be bent down a little, with the legs and the body balanced *(SEE FIGURE 36)*. This is so you are ready to move in any direction, very quickly. Keep the dribbling hand on top of the ball, and keep the head up. When an opponent confronts you, keep your body between the opponent and the ball. Mostly "Point Guards", and "Shooting Guards", need to work on this drill.

Practice:

To practice this drill you, mom or dad, go out to the driveway, or on the court. Then have your son or daughter get about 5 or 6 yards away from you. Have them slowly start to dribble right at you. When they start their dribble, you go slowly right towards them and confront them. What they have to do is, turn away from you, protect the ball, and try to slowly dribble around, or away from, you. Observe and make sure they stay low, pivot their body away from you as they go by, and keep their hand on top of the ball. Have them come at you first from your left, with a right handed dribble. Try that a few times, then have them move over to the other side, and come at you with a left handed dribble.

Hesitate or Stutter Step Dribble

The Basics are:

In this type of dribble, the dribbler comes at an opponent at a fast dribble. When they get a few yards away from the opponent, they

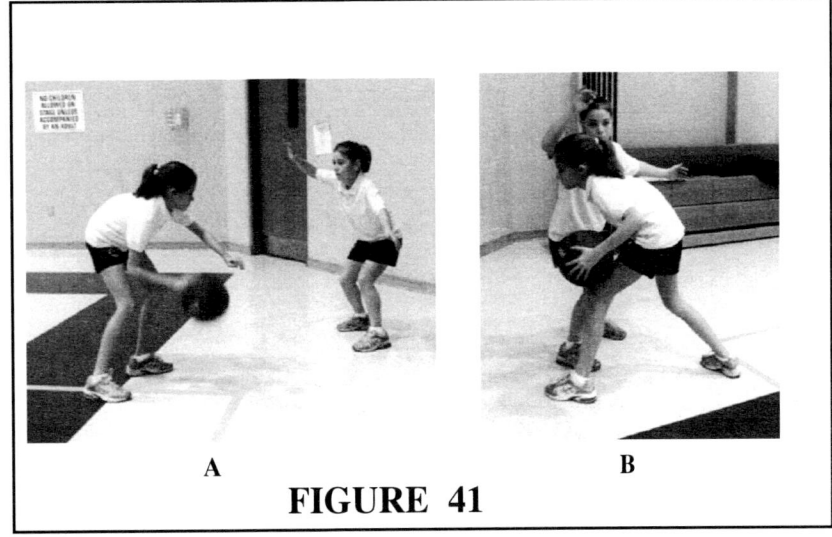

FIGURE 41

slow down very quickly (the hesitate) and take 3 or 4 short (the stutter) choppy steps *(SEE FIGURE 41-A)*. At this point, don't let the ball come up higher than your hip. The opponent thinks you are going to slow down, so they slow down. The stutter step is actually a faking move. Then all of a sudden, you stay low and fast break explode around them, staying close to them. Then shielding the ball with your body as you go by *(SEE FIGURE 41-B)*. Mostly "Point Guards", and "Shooting Guards", need to work on this drill.

Practice:

To practice this drill you, mom or dad, go out to the driveway, or on the court. Then have your son or daughter get about 6 or 7 yards away from you. Have them start to dribble very fast right at you. When they start their dribble, you go slowly right towards them, and confront them. What they have to do is, get up to about 8 feet away from you, then slow down quickly. They keep the ball low, no higher than their hip. Next they keep dribbling the ball, but they take 3 or 4 short choppy steps with the feet. This is where the feet speed up, but the dribble speed stays the same. Then all of a sudden, they fast break explode dribble around you. Since they are the one practicing, you have to stand there and let them get by. Observe and make sure they stay low, pivot their body away from you as they go by, and keep their hand on top of the ball. Also make sure they stay very close to you as they go by. Have them come at you first from your right, with a left handed dribble. Try that a few times, then have them move over to the other side, and come at you with a right handed dribble. The stutter step is going to be hard for the younger kids to learn. So walk them through it slowly until they catch onto the technique.

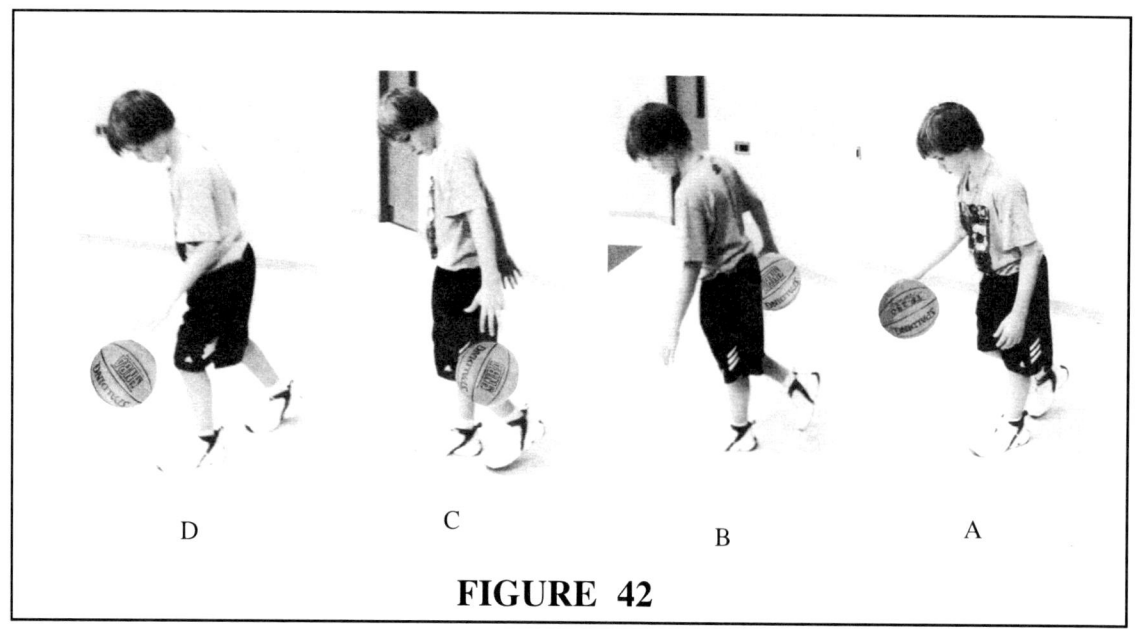

D C B A

FIGURE 42

Behind the Back Dribble

The Basics are:

You are dribbling along *(SEE FIGURE 42-A)*, then suddenly you push the ball around behind your back, just after it bounces up to your dribble hand *(SEE FIGURE 42-B)*. You execute the rest of this move, by catching it with the other hand as the ball comes around your back to the other side, then bounces up *(SEE FIGURE 41-C)*, so you can keep right on dribblng the ball with the left hand *(SEE FIGURE 42-D)*. If you are right handed, you push the ball around your waist, to in back of your left hip. If you are left handed, then just the opposite, you push it around with the left hand. Have your son or daughter learn to practice this move without looking. Its not easy to do, so it will take a lot of practice. It has to be accomplished mostly by feel, and trial and error attempts. Start when they are young, and keep working with them until they master this technique. Mostly "Point Guards", and "Shooting Guards", need to work on this drill.

Practice:

To practice this drill, you will need to find a court, or at least a flat driveway to work on. It's probably best to *"walk"* your son or daughter through this first, just so they get the feel of what is required. Start by having them go down to one end of the court, or driveway. First have them take the ball with the right hand, then step out with the left foot, and at the same time start to dribble the ball once with the right hand. Next as they start to step out with the right foot, and the ball comes up into the hand, you grasp it with a cupped hand and fingers, from on top of the ball. Then you roll push it behind your back. As it comes around, you push it downward at an angle, and let it drop to the floor just outside of your left thigh. Some coaches like to call this a "slap your left butt cheek" action. Then as the ball is about to hit the floor, you start to step forward with your left foot. And then when the ball bounces up, you catch it with the left hand and dribble it down once. Next when it comes back up, you roll it back around your back with the left hand, just like with the righthand. The object is to move slowly straight down the court, switching hands as you go behind your back. What you want to eventually do in this drill is, get a fluid motion going. One dribble on the right, then behind your back, one dribble on the left, then behind your back. You should be doing this as you walk forward, all the way down the court. When they have mastered this technique, you can have them speed up the drill, little by little. It will take many hours, and lots of patience on your part mom or dad, to teach them to perform this move smoothly. It's one of the hardest moves to learn, in basketball. And some kids may never learn how to do it until they get older. If they get real fustrated, just quit working on this drill and come back to it later. Even if they can't learn this move, they can still be a good "Point Guard", or a "Shooting Guard".

Switch Hands Crossover Dribble

The Basics are:

Dribbling the ball down court, switching it from one side to the other, and then from one hand to the other. When you have mastered this technique, it can be done at moderate to high speed. Changing pace while executing this dribbling move, will confuse and fool the opponent also. When dribbled, the ball needs to be pushed down keeping it close to the body, and always toward the back foot side. And as you push the ball across, keep it no higher than the top of the knee. Another part of this technique is, changing direction along with the crossover. This move is used to get around an opponent, from back court to the middle of the court. Mostly "Point Guards", "Shooting Guards", and Small Forwards", need to work on this drill.

Practice:

To practice this drill, you will need to find a court, or at least a flat driveway to work on. It's probably best to *"walk"* your son or daughter through this first, just so they get the feel of what is required. Start by having them go down to one end of the court, or driveway. First have them take the ball with the right hand,

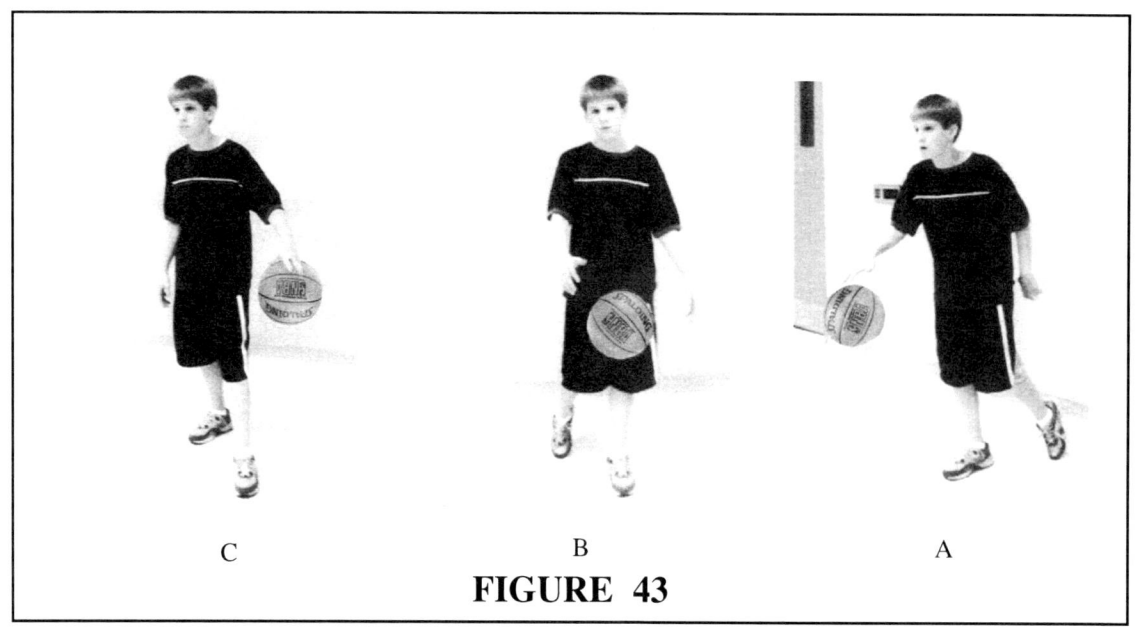

FIGURE 43

then step out with the right foot *(SEE FIGURE 43-A)*. And next, at the same time, dribble push the ball in one dribble, across the front of your body *(SEE FIGURE 43-B)*, so it comes up to your left hand. Your left foot should hit the floor as you step out with the ball, just as the ball has come up to your left hand *(SEE FIGURE 43-C)*. Next repeat the move, from your left hand bouncing it across to your right hand. Then keep repeating the move, back and forth as you walk down the court. With the young kids, they can look down at the ball until they master the technique. Eventually though you need to speed up the drill, all the way down the court, little by little as they get better at performing the move. And they should also work towards *not* looking at the ball while making this move. The key is perfecting the footwork, timing, and speed of the move.

Through the Legs Dribble

The Basics are:

The through the legs dribble is really a variation of the crossover dribble. The ball is pushed between the legs, instead of in front of the body. When it comes out the other side, you start to dribble with the other hand, then go in the opposite direction. You need to bend down and stay low, just before you push the ball between your legs. A little head fake, off to the side "opposite" of where you really want to go, will help the move be even more successful. In a way though this move may be a better choice than the crossover dribble move because even if the opponent is close to you, it's harder for them to reach the ball when it goes between the legs. And it's a good change of pace move, in the front

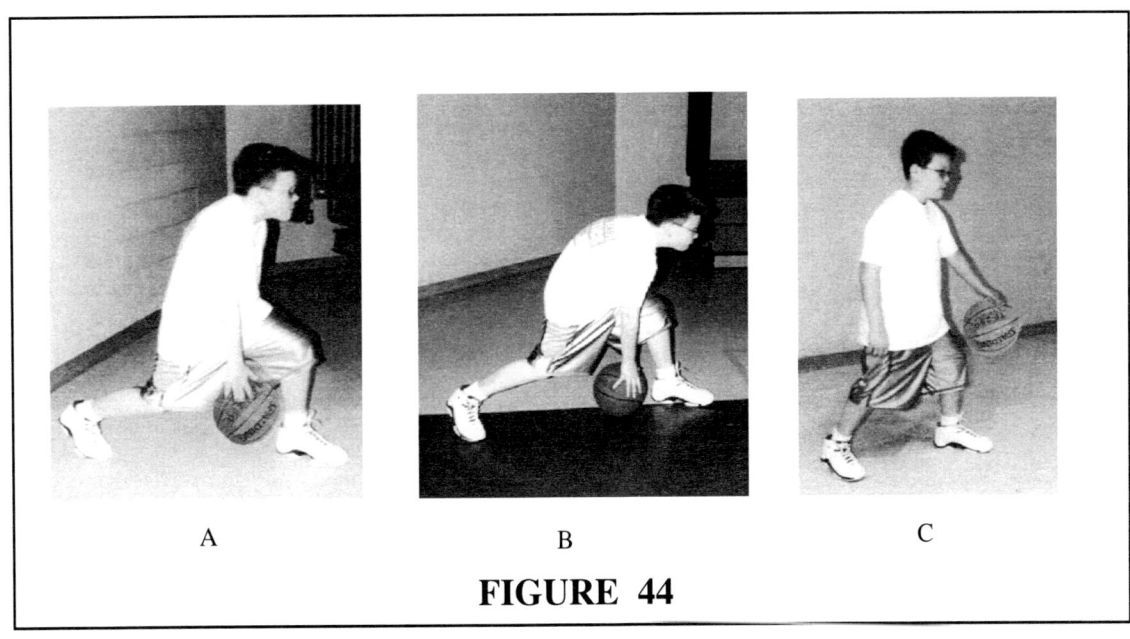

FIGURE 44

court, to get you into the lane for a shot. Mostly "Point Guards", and "Shooting Guards", need to work on this drill.

Practice:

To practice this drill, you will need to find a court, or at least a flat driveway to work on. It's probably best to *"walk"* your son or daughter through this first, just so they get the feel of what is required. You can have them speed things up, little by little as the get better, and more comfortable with the technique. There are several ways to make this move. Have your son or daughter try out both ways, then start out using the one that is easiest for them to execute.

The first is, start by having them go down to one end of the court, or driveway. Have them take the ball with the right hand, then as they start to dribble, step out with their left foot at about a 45 degree angle towards their left **SEE FIGURE 44-A)**. Stay low with the knees bent a little. Next just as your left foot is about to hit the floor, bounce push the ball under and through the left leg **(SEE FIGURE 44-B)**. While you are doing this, place your left hand behind you, with the palm facing your back. This is so you are ready to catch the ball as it comes through. Then just as you are catching the ball, with your left hand, step forward and to the right, at a 45 degree angle with your right foot. This is to make room, for a smooth transition of the ball under your legs. Then you bring the ball around your left foot, and start to dribble off to your left **(SEE FIGURE 44-C)**. This move will be a little unnatural for them when they start, but keep working at it until they get used to it. This is the better of the two moves if you want to change the direction you are going in. Next dribble the ball several times as you are dribbling and walking, then reverse the process and bounce push the ball back under your legs to the right hand. Keep doing this back and forth all the way down the court. Two or three dribbles, then change hands.

The second is, start by having them go down to one end of the court, or driveway. Have them take the ball with the right hand, then as you start to dribble, take a big step straight ahead with your left foot *(SEE FIGURE 44-A)*. At the same time bend the right leg down at the knee. Next bounce push the ball under and through the left leg *(SEE FIGURE 44-B)*. At the same time place the left hand, with the palm down, next to your left thigh. This is to catch the ball with the left hand as it comes up. Then as you step straight ahead with the right foot, you bring the ball around your left foot, and start to dribble off straight ahead. Except now the ball is on your left side away from the opponent *(SEE FIGURE 44-C)*. This is the best move if you want to keep going basically straight ahead, and keep the ball away from your opponent who is on your right side. Next dribble the ball several times as you are dribbling and walking, then reverse the process, and bounce push the ball back under your legs to the right hand. Keep doing this, back and forth, all the way down the court. Two or three dribbles, then change hands.

Spin Move Dribble

The Basics are:

The spin move dribble is a spin around, change direction move. While you are dribbling straight ahead, you spin around in a reverse pivot. Then change to the opposite hand as you go around, and then go off in another direction. The ball should be kept close to the body, and swing the head around fast. Mostly "Point Guards", "Shooting Guards", and Small Forwards", need to work on this drill.

Practice:

To practice this drill, you will need to find a court, or at least a flat driveway to work on. It's probably best to *"walk"* your son or daughter through this first, just so they get the feel of what is required. You can have them speed things up little by little as the get better, and more comfortable with the technique.

Start by having them go down to one end of the court, or driveway. Have them take the ball with the right hand, then as they start to dribble slowly towards you, they take one jab step right at you with the left foot as they get about 6 feet away *(SEE FIGURE 46-A)*. Next they have to stop very quickly, reverse pivot spin around to their right. The spin around should go about 3/4 of the way

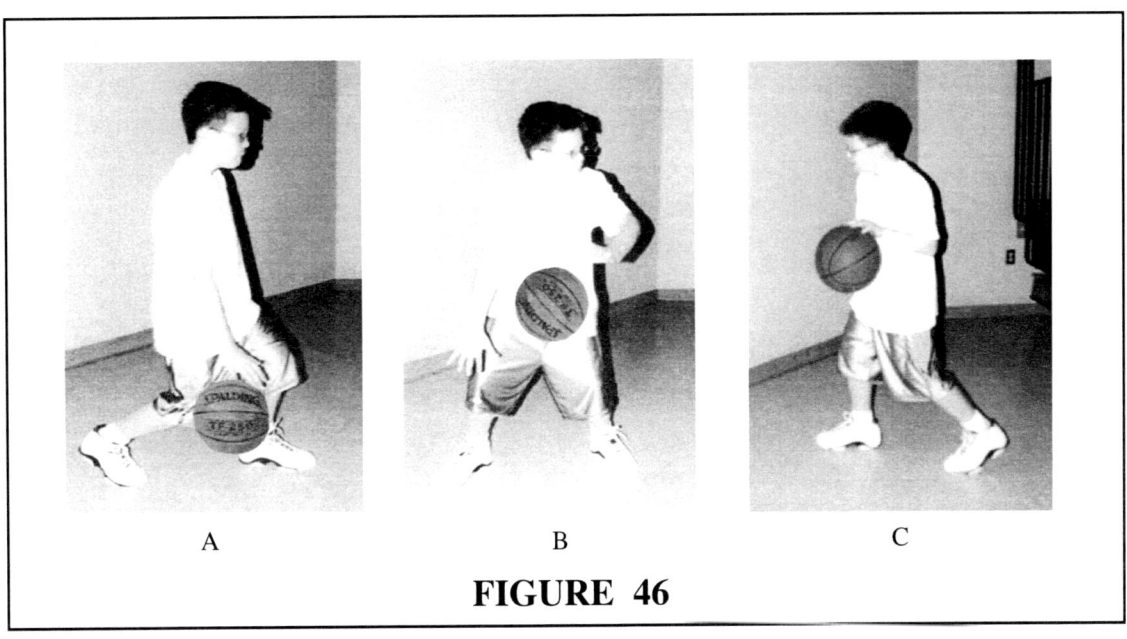

FIGURE 46

around. As they spin, they keep the ball close to the body *(SEE FIGURE 46-B)*. And the head spin around should be done very quickly, almost a snapping motion. When they start the spin around, they push the ball down, then they spin and catch it with the left hand *(SEE FIGURE 46-B)* as it comes up fom the dribble. Then they continue the spin while dribbling off to the left at a slight angle with the left hand *(SEE FIGURE-C)*. Next dribble the ball several times in the left hand as you are dribbling and walking down the court, then reverse the process, jab step with the right foot, spin around to your left, and change the dribble to the right hand. Keep doing this, back and forth, all the way down the court. Two or three dribbles, spin, then change hands. To make this work the spin has to executed very fast.

Shuffle Dribble

The Basics are:
The shuffle dribble is sort of a straight ahead, sliding, advancing, shuffle move, first with one foot then the other while dribbling the ball. You remember the phrase "Inching ahead cautiously". Well that is kind of like what this is, except you are going a little farther than inching. This would be a move you might use in the front court, to kind of slowly move toward the basket when the opponent is fronting you, but backed off a little bit. Mostly "Point Guards", "Shooting Guards", and Small Forwards", need to work on this drill.

Practice:

To practice this drill, you will need to find a court, or at least a flat driveway to work on. It's probably best to *"walk"* your son or daughter through this first, just so they get the feel of what is required. You can have them speed things up, little by little as the get better, and feel more comfortable with the technique.

Start by having them go down to one end of the court, or driveway. Have them stand straight up, with feet apart about shoulder width. Your left foot and your head should be pointing straight ahead. Then rotate your body to the right until your left shoulder is pointing straight ahead also. Turn the right foot 90 degrees, so it is pointing to the right. Next bend at the knees to about a 45 degree angle to the floor, and widen your stance out about another 6 inches. Then move the left arm straight out from your body at about a 45 degree angle, then bend the forearm so it is at a right angle from the upper arm. Take the ball in your right hand. At this point, they are ready to start shuffle dribbling down the court *(SEE FIGURE 47-A)*. Make sure their knees are bent, and they dribble no higher than the knees. The point they bounce the ball on the dribble, should be halfway between the front foot and the back foot. One more thing, the forefinger on the dribble hand should be pointed in the direction you are shuffling. Start to dribble with the right hand, and at the same time slide step out with your left foot *(SEE FIGURE 47-B)*. The second the left foot stops, slide step straight ahead with the turned right foot, bringing it up close to the left foot while still pointing it to the right *(SEE FIGURE 47-C)*. All this time, you are bent low and dribbling the ball. Do this straight ahead for about 4 or 5 steps, then switch to a left handed dribble. Turn the shoulder to the right, and do the same shuffle step

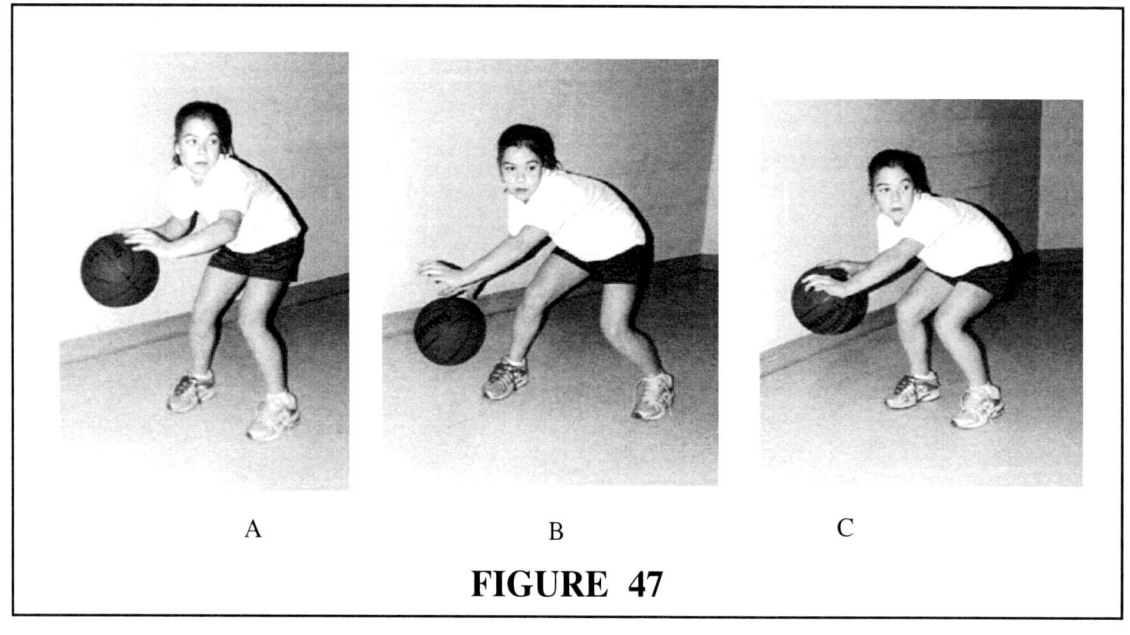

A   B   C

FIGURE 47

leading with the right foot, for about 4 or 5 steps. Keep doing this, from one side to the other, all the way down the court. 4 or 5 shuffle steps, turn the opposite way, change hands, 4 or 5 shuffle steps, turn the opposite way, change hands, and so on.

Stop and Go Dribble

The Basics are:
This dribble is a variation of the "fast high speed dribble". The difference is when you are moving fast down the court, and an opponent is guarding you fairly close, you would suddenly come to stop as quickly as possible. Then just as you come to the complete stop, you explode out again quickly and either dribble, shoot, or pass the ball. What happens is when you stop very quickly, the rapid change of pace tends to stop the opponent "in his tracks", so to speak, and that will free up enough space for you to make the next dribble move, shot, or pass. Mostly "Point Guards", "Shooting Guards", and Small Forwards", need to work on this drill.

Practice:
To practice this drill, you will need to find a court, or at least a large flat driveway, or even a parking lot, to practice on. It's probably best to *"walk"* your son or daughter through this first, just so they get the feel of what is required. You can have them speed things up, little by little as the get better, and feel more comfortable with the technique.

We will use the basketball court as our guide. However if you don't have a court to use, then mark off equivalent distances with cones. Start by having them go down to one end of the court on the base line, or end of the driveway, or a marked off place with cones on the parking lot. Have them start with a fast high speed dribble, going down court *(SEE FIGURE 48-A)*. What you want to have them do is, make "stops" at the two free throw lines, the center court line, and the other base line. As they approach one of these stop points, and they are dribbling with the right hand, then they brake when the left foot is out in front. At the same time they change to a lower dribble, lower their center of gravity, and distribute their body weight to both feet. And also at this same time, bring the dribble right next to, and slightly in front of your right knee. Keep the head up and the back straight, which helps make the stop *(SEE FIGURE 48-B)*. Just as you stop, lower the dribble to knee high or lower. The dribble hand should be in line with the shoulder, and the forefinger on the dribble hand should be pointing

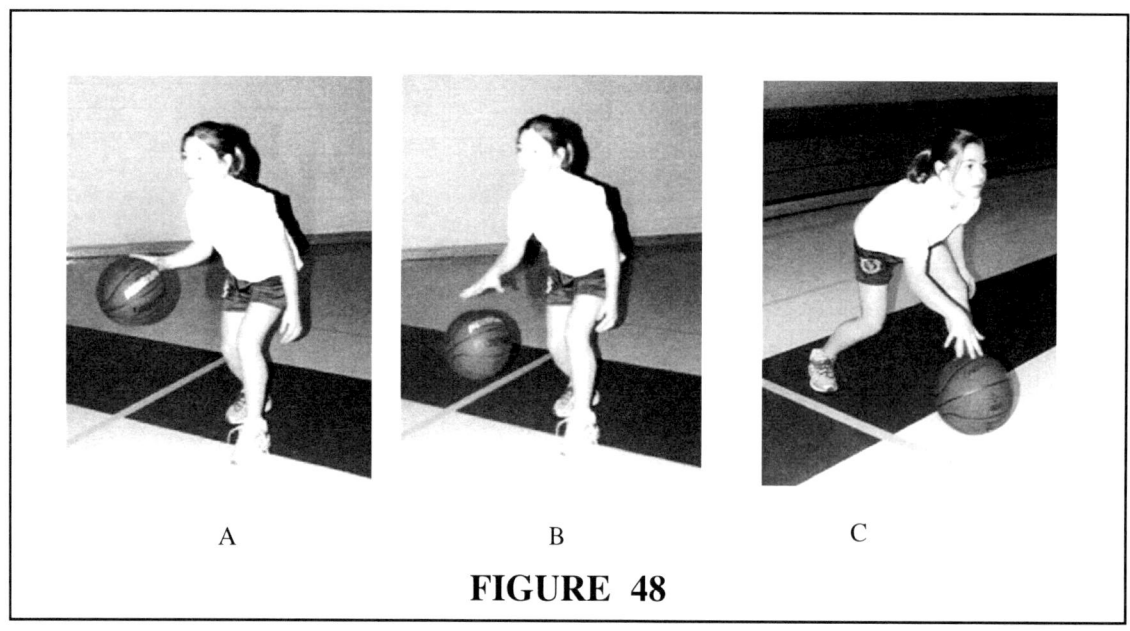

FIGURE 48

straight ahead. A tip here as you stop, push the ball straight down, and the ball should come straight back up to your hand, and not get away from you.

Now just as you get to a complete "stop" at the first free throw line, you execute a "go", explode, high speed, fast break type dribble, to the center line *(SEE FIGURE 48-C)*. "Stop" there, then execute the "go" technique, all the way to the next free throw line. Again "stop" there, then execute another "go" technique, all the way to the upcoming base line. Then stop and turn around. All of this has been with the right hand. Next go all the way back, dribbling with the left hand. Make your "stop's", and "go's", at the same points going back.

Change of Pace Dribble

The Basics are:

The change of pace dribble is a variation of the "stop and go" dribble. If you dribble at a constant speed, it is easier for the opponent to guard you. All they have to do is match your speed, and they stay right with you. So what you do is vary the rate of speed of the dribble. When they match your speed, you slow down quickly when they slow down you speed up quickly. I have heard some people call this the "Yo-Yo effect". Mostly "Point Guards", "Shooting Guards", and Small Forwards", need to work on this drill.

Practice:

To practice this drill, you will need to find a court, or at least a large flat driveway, or even a parking lot, to practice on. It's probably best to *"walk"* your son or daughter through this first, just so they get the feel of what is required. You can have them speed things up, little by little as the get better, and feel more comfortable with the technique.

We will use the basketball court as our guide. However if you don't have a court to use, then mark off equivalent distances with cones. Start by having them go down to one end of the court on the base line, or end of the driveway, or a marked off place with cones on the parking lot. Have them start with a fast high speed "right" handed dribble, going down court *(SEE FIGURE 48-A)*. And you, mom or dad, get right next to them, but not too close, and try to match the speed at which they are moving. What you want to have them do is, all of a sudden after dribbling about 5 yards down court, have them slow down very quickly, but don't come to a stop *(SEE FIGURE 48-B)*. You slow down with them. What they have to do is watch you, and when they see you slow down, they speed up *(SEE FIGURE 48-C)*. Then you speed up, and try to stay next to them. Again they have to watch you, out of the corner of their eyes. When they see that you are really coming hard to catch them, they slow down and let you catch them, then when you slow down again, they speed up again. This goes on all the way down to the other base line. The object is to keep you from staying right along side of them where you could reach in and knock the ball away from them. Now, both of you stop at the base line, turn around, and have them go down the court doing the same thing the other way, except dribbling this time with their "left" hand. The tip here is, keep doing this over and over again. In other words, practice, practice, practice.

Drills for Catching

Drill No. 24- Toughen the Hands

The Basics are:
Many coaches say a players hands have to be tough because of all the handling of the basketball, during practices and games. Part of this is, the fingers need to be flexible. Sensitivity is also important. That is you must feel the ball without looking at it. This applies to all players.

Practice:
One of the things some coaches have their players do is, take the basketball in one hand and slam it hard into the other hand, then take it in that hand and

slam it back to the other hand, over and over, back and forth *(SEE FIGURE 49)*. Sometimes this is refered to as the "Pound Drill". Try and have them do this every day, for at least a few minutes.

For the fingers, have them do at least a few minutes of "finger flexing" every day. They can do this sitting, or standing. While they are watching TV is another good time for this drill. What they do is extend both hands out in front of them. Then open up and spread all the fingers, with the palms facing each other. Then just squeeze each hand together, making a fist *(SEE FIGURE 50)*. Next open up all the fingers back to the starting position. Then make a fist again. And just keep doing this, over and over again, for several minutes every day.

FIGURE 49

Drill No. 25- Catching the Basketball

The Basics are:

When catching the ball, they should have both arms extended, palms facing the incoming pass, with the fingers spread out. The thumbs should be about 2 inches apart, and the fingers should be up if the ball comes in at chest heigth *(SEE FIGURE 51-A)*. If the ball comes in at knee to waist heigth, the fingers should be down, and the thumbs outward *(SEE FIGURE 51-B)*. Once the ball is in the air, <u>look</u> it into your hands. Next you should step toward the incoming pass, and bend the knees a little bit. Step with the left foot if you are right handed, step with the right foot if you are left handed. And as it hits your hands, bring the hands into the body. **<u>Do Not</u>** point your fingers straight at the ball because you could

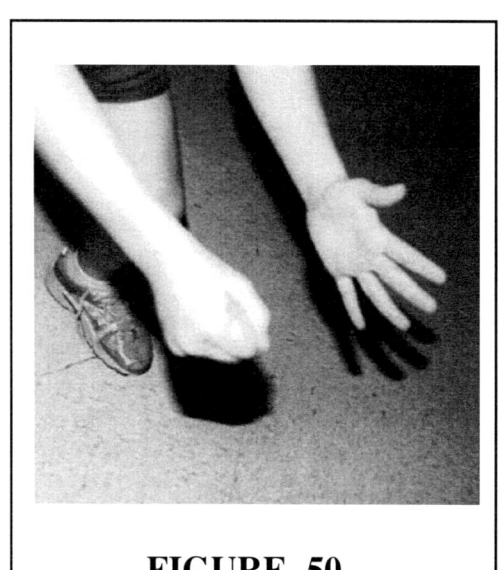

FIGURE 50

sprain, dislocate, or even break a finger. The arms and elbows need to be flexible, to absorb the shock of the ball hitting the hands. If you lock the elbows, and stiffen the arms, the ball will probably bounce off your hands and onto the floor. All players need to work on this

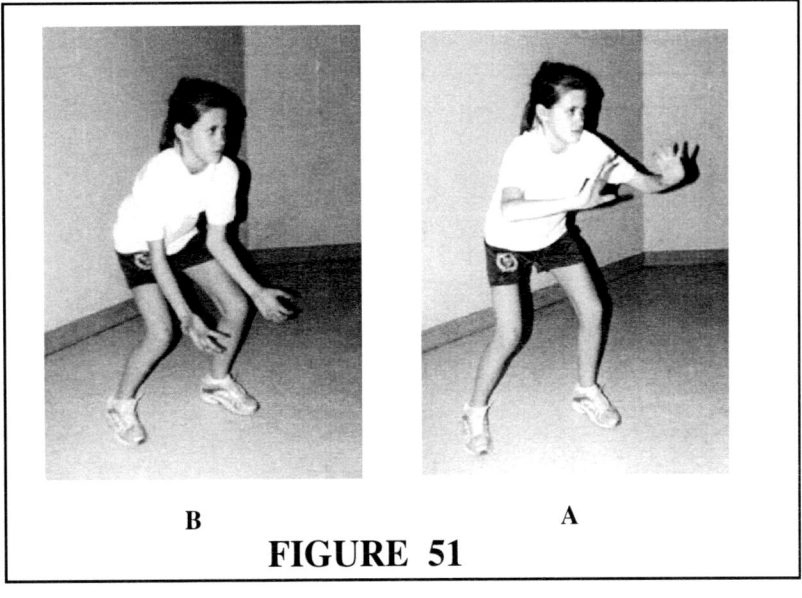

FIGURE 51

drill. The _TIP_ is keep the fingers loose, and flexible.

Practice:

To practice this drill you, mom or dad, take the basketball, go out to the driveway and get about 7 yards away from your son or daughter. Have them get into a ready stance *(SEE FIGURE 52)*. Then pass them the ball, sometimes chest high, and sometimes knee to waist high. Observe and make sure their fingers are pointing the right way, for the heigth of the ball as it gets to them. Also check and make sure they don't get into a habit of pointing any fingers at the ball. Even doing this drill 3 to 5 minutes every day will help. The minute they catch the ball, they pass it right back to you. This will letthem get in more repetitions, in a short period of time.

Drills for Faking

Drill No. 26- Offensive Faking

The Basics are:

Using faking moves is an age old technique. It has been probably been around since the first years of basketball. It envolves using the head and shoulders. The object is to get the opponent out of position, to let you continue to dribble, pass,

FIGURE 52

63

or shoot. By shifting, turning, or dipping the head, makes the opponent think you are going to do something you are not going to do. The same thing applies with the shoulders. A clever player can even use the knee, or the feet, to fool an opponent. Dipping the knee in one direction, then sfifting the body, pivoting, and pushing off in the other direction with the lead foot, can get the opponent leaning the wrong way. The stutter step is a foot fake. All players should learn how to fake, but mostly "Point Guards", "Shooting Guards", and Small Forwards", need to work on this drill.

Practice:

Go out to the court or driveway and you, mom or dad, get about where the free throw line is, with your back to the basket. Then have your son or daughter get in front of you, about 3 feet away, and face you. There are several ways to practice these moves. For the first one, have them get into a "right- agressive" stance *(SEE FIGURE 53-A)*. The pivot can be off of either foot. It depends on how close the opponent is. If the opponent is backed off 2 or 3 feet away, have them shift or dip the head once to the left, then at the same time pivot and turn to the right, off the front foot. The first step is to the right with the right foot. Next they push off on the front foot, fast break around you to their right, and dribble toward the basket for a layup shot *(SEE FIGURE 41-B)*. If the first head fake does not get the opponent leaning away from you, to your left, then you may have to do a double head fake to get them to lean. If the opponent is up real close, and guarding you very tight, you have to do the head fake to get the opponent leaning. Next, you pivot off the back foot, turn to the right, pull the left arm in tight, then crossover step with the front foot. Then they go into a fast break dribble, around you to their right, and go to the basket for a layup shot. To even add more to the fake, have them use the shoulder dip or turn. After they have mastered this

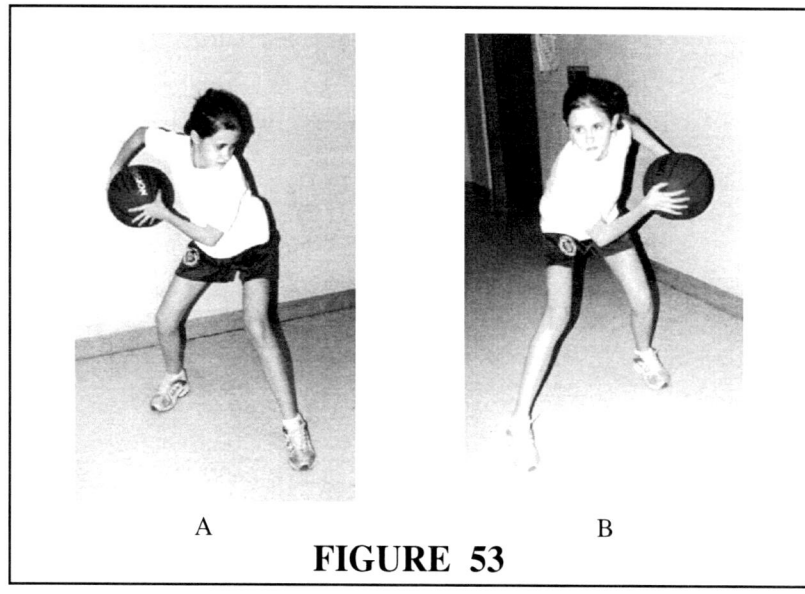

A   B
FIGURE 53

to the right, have them go into a "left- agressive" stance *(SEE FIGURE 53-B)*. Then have them do the head and shoulder fakes to their right, to get the opponent leaning left. When they get you to lean, they fast break around you to their left, for a layup shot.

Second, for some variations off of the stance, get a third party helper and position them off to the side, right or left. Then have them get you to lean, and pass the ball to the helper. And by the way, mom or dad, always be sure to lean, or start to step, in the direction they are faking you. You know what they are going to do, but this is so they can see, and learn, what the result of the fake looks like.

Third they can also practice a jump shot off the fake *(SEE FIGURE 67)*. Remember though don't try the jump shot off the fake if the opponent is guarding you very tight. The reason is you will probably foul them with your arm. Most kids can't execute a fade away jumper yet, so wait till they are older to try it. So, mom or dad, back off at least 3 or 4 feet away, let them fake you, then try their jump shot.

Fourth they can try some knee fakes. Lots of coaches don't like to teach kids to do this. It does not mean they have to use this technique, but they should at least know what it is like. What you have to do is bend, and dip, the knee down and up very fast, on the leading leg, to get the opponent leaning. Have them get into the right- agressive stance *(SEE FIGURE 53-A)*. Next have them do a very fast dip with the left knee. Then quickly bring it right back. However, let me point out here that both feet have to always stay planted (can pivot but not lift off the floor). If they get the opponent to lean to their left (and of course you will , mom or dad), they pivot, turn and fast break around them to the right, just like in the head and shoulder fakes. Sometimes it may take a short delay, then a second dip, to get the opponent to lean. Some kids may never learn faking, but at least show them what it is, and let them try it. I personally think its natural for some young kids, and not others.

The stutter step is a foot faking technique that a player can use, to make a play *(SEE FIGURE 41)*.

Another important thing to point out here if you see that you are about to be double teamed, or you are in a croud, don't bother to do any faking. Pass the ball off because that means one of your team mates must be wide open, and in the clear.

Drill No. 27- Defensive Faking

The Basics are:

When you are on defense, there are also fakes that can be made. They can be head, shoulder, or foot fakes. You would execute these fakes almost like the offensive fakes, except for different reasons, and with some exceptions. Defensive players are not held to the same "traveling" rules as the offensive player. By that I mean with the feet. They can pivot off of one or both feet, jump up, or make about any kind of move they like as long as they don't touch the offensive player for a foul. Defensive players fake to make the offensive player think they are going to shift in one direction, when they really want to shift the other way, to block the opponents move to the basket. What they are really doing is setting the offensive player up, so they can get a charging foul called. This way the defender makes the move the way he wants to go, instead of waiting for the offensive player to make the move. The defender does not know what the offensive player wants to do, so they trick the offensive player into going right where they want them to go.

They might also use a head and arms fake, to make the opponent think they are going to jump up to block a shot, or go for a rebound. That usually causes the offensive player to "freeze" for just a moment or two, and that's when you can try for a steal. When you hear the phrase "They have him in the Pop Corn Machine", well that's what this is about. The offensive player pretends to go for a jump shot, right in front of the defender. The object is to get the defender to jump up to block the shot, then when he comes back down, at that moment is when the offensive player times his jump, so they get up in the air without the defenders hands in their face. But sometimes each player is trying to fake the other, so one goes up, one comes down, and this action is like pop corn poping off. All players need to work on these fakes.

Practice:

To practice these techniques go out to the court or driveway, have your son or daughter go to about where the free throw line is, with their back to the basket, and take the ready stance *(SEE FIGURE 52)*. Then you, mom or dad, take the basketball and get in front of them, about 6 feet away, and face them. Next, mom or dad, start to dribble at them slowly, and watch their eyes and head. What they want to do is, head and eye fake like they are going to their left. When you see them do this, dribble slowly around them to your left, then try to go to the basket. What they do next is slide shuffle step back, and to their right, far enough to block your dribble to the basket *(SEE FIGURE 54-A)*. As they slide over, charge straight into them a few times, so they can feel what it is like. Do it in slow motion though so no one gets hurt. In fact you may want to walk through it first, so they know what to do. And just when they see you are going to charge straight into them, they should raise both arms straight up *(SEE FIGURE 54-B)*. Next as contact with you is made, they sit down, arms still up, and slide backwards on the floor *(SEE FIGURE 54-C)*. This has to be on a gym floor, not an asphalt driveway though. The sit down and slide have to be a good acting job, so the foul will be called on the offensive player. Make sure they do all the faking very fast.

Do this drill a few times, then have them head and eye fake, like they are going the other way to their right. Then you take the fake, and try to dribble around them to your right. What they do this time is slide shuffle step back, and to their left, far enough to block your dribble to the basket, going around the opposite way.

To practice the fake jump up, both of you go back out to the same place you were for the "slide shuffle" fake. Then you, mom or dad, take one step then pretend to go up for a jump shot. Your son or daughter has to watch you very carefully, then the second you start to move the arm up for a shot, they pretend to jump up in front of you to block the shot *(SEE FIGURE 55-A)*. When you see that they appear to start a jump up for the block, you just stop and freeze where you are. While you are doing all this, they have to only watch the ball. So when you freeze, they need to very quickly step in and grab the ball *(SEE FIGURE 55-B)*. Try this a few times, and let them steal the ball. Make sure

C   B   A

FIGURE 54

FIGURE 55

they are selling you on the fake though before you let them make the steal. This is so they can see what happens when they don't sell the fake to the opponent, and are just standing there flat footed waiting. What they <u>*do not*</u> want to do is, reach in and hit your hand for a foul. It has to be a clean grab, going very quickly for the ball. The grab can be with two hands if they are close enough. Or they can just try to knock the ball away, with one hand. Sometimes though, mom or dad, go for the jump shot up over the top of them. Then see what they do. Hopefully if they are watching the ball, like they should be, they will recover and go for the block *(SEE FIGURE 55-C)*.

Drills for Footwork

Here are some thoughts on footwork. One of the great all time basketball coaches said "A player will only handle the ball maybe 10 percent of the time", but they will use their feet 100 percent of the time. So genreally speaking, pay a lot of attention to the footwork on <u>***each***</u> drill, it's very important. We will cover some of the basic footwork now being taught for the "ready stance", making cuts, pivots, and the jump stop (for the jump shot).

Drill No. 28- Ready Stance

The Basics are:
This position, the ready stance, is the basis for most moves like, starting to

dribble, shoot, pass, catch, jump, guard, and slide defend. Feet should be a little wider than shoulder width, knees bent, with thighs parallel to the floor. The back should be almost straight, and maybe a little forward. Head straight looking forward, hands out in front, with palms facing forward at about shoulder heigth. The fingers should be spread and pointing up. The arms are about halfway bent and the elbows in a little *(SEE FIGURE 52)*. Some coaches refer to this as the "triple threat" stance or position. All players need to work on this stance.

Practice:

This is where working on the "wall sits" strengthening drill No. 14, is going to come in handy. Their thighs should be strong enough to stay in this position for extended periods of time. What you can do, mom or dad, is go out to the court or driveway, and have your son or daughter go out by the sidewalk. Then you get up by the garage door, or an equivalent distance away. Then say "GO",and have them start to slowly run at you. When they get about 6 feet away, have them get quickly into the "ready stance". Then you, mom or dad, point your arm to the right, and they start to slide shuffle side step in that direction, staying in the ready position. Have them go over about 8 or 10 feet, then you change and point to the left. They have to react, change direction quickly, and go the other way about 8 to 10 feet. Then say "STOP", and have them return to the starting point out by the sidewalk. Keep doing this, over and over, several times until it becomes a habit to them.

There are several other things you could also do with them, to practice this stance. You could have them stand out at the free throw line. Then you, mom or dad, stand up by the garage door, or an equivalent distance, and say "GO". They would then go into the "ready stance", then you pass them the ball. They catch the ball, still in their stance, then they step out with the left foot, and pass the ball quickly back to you. Go back into their stance, and get ready to catch the ball again. Keep doing this, back and forth, as fast as you both can, sort of like a baseball game of "pepper".

Here is another practice technique you could use. Have them stand at the free throw line, say "GO", and have them quickly get into the "ready stance". Then you, mom or dad, pass them the ball. They catch the ball, then take a step or two and make a jump shot at the basket. After that they go quickly back to the starting point. Next you catch, or rebound, the ball and pass it quickly back to them. So you kind of get a little game of "pepper" going (as fast as you can get the ball back to them and they can shoot).

Drill No. 29- Making Cuts

The Basics are:
　　During a game, players make a lot of stops, then cuts to one side or the other, to get into an open position. The footwork is what gets you around the opponent. Lets say a team mate passes you the ball, and you want to get open on the left side of the court. You would first get into an "agressive stance" *(SEE FIGURE 53-B)*. Next you would stay low, reverse pivot,

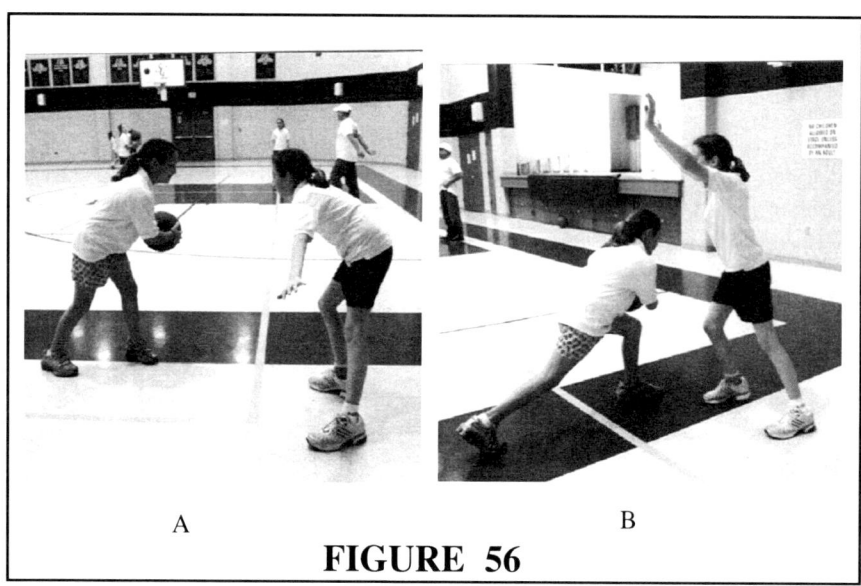

A　　　　　　　　　　B
FIGURE 56

and push off with the right foot. Next you would turn to the left *(SEE FIGURE 56-A)*, and start to dribble around the left side of the opponent, using an explode type move *(SEE FIGURE 56-B)*. Getting open on the right side of the court is just the opposite. Everything is reversed, you pivot on the left foot, and explode dribble around the opponents right side. Make sure to teach them to cut both left and right. All players should learn how to make cuts, but mostly "Point Guards", "Shooting Guards", and Small Forwards", need to work on this drill.

Practice:
　　To practice this drill, you will need to find a court, or at least a flat driveway to work on. It's probably best to *"walk"* your son or daughter through this first, just so they get the feel of what is required. You can have them speed things up, little by little as the get better, and more comfortable with the technique.
　　Start by giving them the basketball then you, mom or dad, go out about 5 feet in front of them. Have them get into a "right- aggressive" stance *(SEE FIGURE 53-A)*. Then say "GO", and have them explode cut around you. First going right, then practice going left. Put your hands up to guard them, but let them get around you. As you are guarding them, observe and make sure they are using the correct footwork.

Drill No. 30- Making Pivots

The Basics are:

There are basically two kinds of pivots. The "forward pivot", and the "reverse pivot". To execute the forward pivot, you would pivot and turn in a forward direction, off the ball of the front foot *(SEE FIGURE 57-A)*. Keep the ball close to your body to protect it, and stay low and keep your balance. To execute the reverse pivot, you would pivot and turn the other way with the front foot. Lead with the front elbow, then swing the back elbow behind you, on the side opposite the pivot foot *(SEE FIGURE 57-B)*. Pull the ball in to protect it, and stay balanced. All pivots should be executed very aggressively, and very fast. All players should learn how to make pivots, but mostly "Point Guards", "Shooting Guards", and Small Forwards", need to work on this drill.

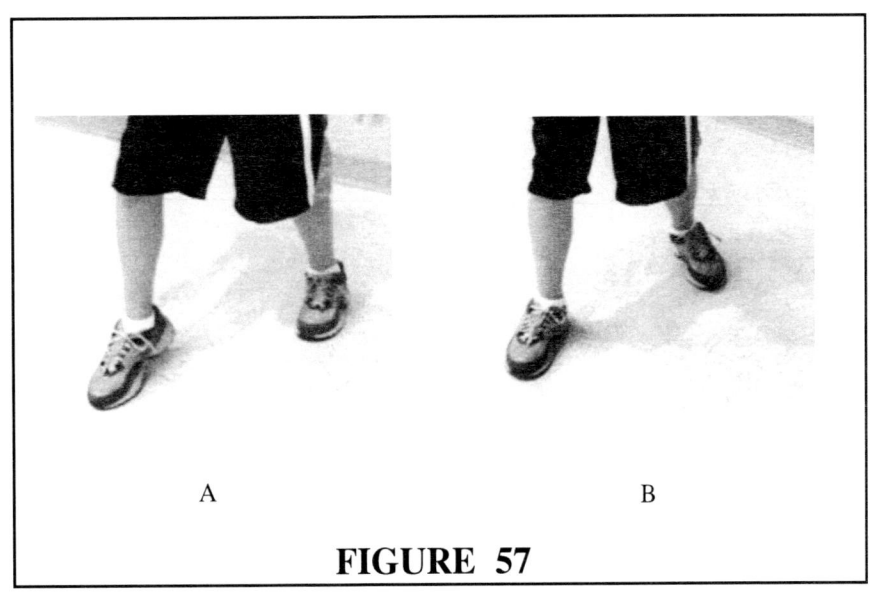

FIGURE 57

Practice:

To practice this drill, you will need to find a court, or at least a flat driveway to work on. It's probably best to *"walk"* your son or daughter through this first, just so they get the feel of what is required. You can have them speed things up little by little as the get better, and more comfortable with the technique.

Start by giving them the basketball then you, mom or dad, go out about 5 feet in front of them, and guard them. Have them get into a "right- aggressive" stance *(SEE FIGURE 53-A)*. Then say "GO", and have them execute a forward pivot, to the left. To do this they need to lift up on the ball of their left foot, pivot, and turn slightly to the left *(SEE FIGURE 57-A)*. Next they step out with the left foot, swing the basketball around to the left, and push off with the right rear foot. Then left hand dribble away, down the court for 6 to 8 feet, then stop.

Then have them go back to the starting point, and get back into their right hand stance. Say "GO" again, and have them execute a reverse pivot to the right. To do this they need to pivot to the right, on the front left foot, then turn to the right. Next they swing the left front elbow around to the right, pulling the ball and the right elbow way around their back *(SEE FIGURE 57-B)*. Then they crossover step in front, with the left foot, and right hand dribble off around to the right for 6 to 8 feet, then stop.

Next have them go back to the starting point, and get into a "left-aggressive" stance *(SEE FIGURE 53-B)*. Then reverse everything, and have them execute a forward pivot, and a reverse pivot, then dribbling down the court for 6 to 8 feet, then stop. Keep doing this over and over until it becomes a habit with them.

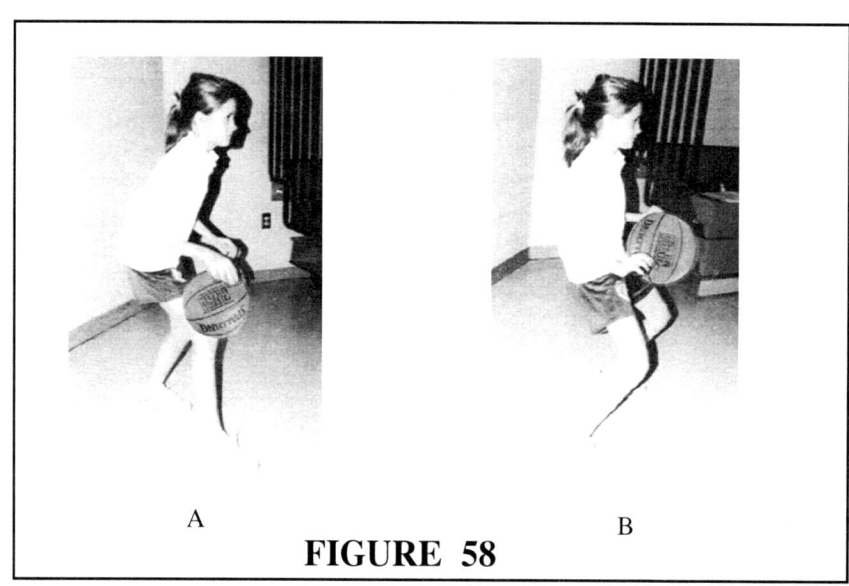

FIGURE 58

Drill No. 31- Making the Jump Stop

The Basics are:

The "jump stop" is the pre-footwork for making the jump shot. To execute a jump stop, from running or dribbling down court, the player takes a short hop *(SEE FIGURE 58-A)*. Then they come down with both feet on the floor at the same time *(SEE FIGURE 58-B)*. When they come down on the floor, the feet should be shoulder width apart, butt low, and the knees bent and flexible. From this position the player can make a jump shot, or go into the ready stance. All players should learn how to make jump stops, but mostly "Point Guards", "Shooting Guards", and Small Forwards", need to work on this drill.

Practice:

To practice this drill, you will need to find a court, or at least a flat driveway to work on. It's probably best to *"walk"* your son or daughter through this first, just so they get the feel of what is required. You can have them speed things up, little by little as the get better, and more comfortable with the technique.

Start by giving them the basketball then you, mom or dad, go out to a spot about 9 feet out in front of the basket. Have your son or daughter go out to a spot, in front of the basket, about at the mid court line, or an equivalent distance. Have them start dribbling right towards you, then they make a short hop just about at the free throw line. Then coming down at the free throw line, with both feet on the floor at the same time. Next when they land, they push off and jump straight up to execute a jump shot, over the top of you, at the basket *(SEE FIGURE 67)*. If it's easier for them, you can have them just run up to the free throw line, and execute the jump stop, without using the basketball. Have them keep working on this drill, either way until they master this footwork technique.

Drills for Jumping

Jumping is very important in basketball. Kids need to work on jumping when they are little in order to learn how to elevate their center of gravity. In other words, how to improve on their ability to get higher up in the air while playing basketball. This is not easy to do. But if they start working on it when they are 5 years old, they will be a lot better at it when they get to 12 years old. Here are a few drills that will be easy for you to set up at home, to help your son or daughters jumping ability.

Drill No. 32- Over the Broomstick

The Basics are:
Jumping over an object will train the leg muscles, to get you way up in the air. This drill is not very complicated, but it should help them some with getting the feeling of getting up in the air. Just take a regular broom, and use the handle as a bar, for them to get their feet over. You hold the broom, and have them stand stationary about 18 inches in front of the broom handle. Next, in one jump, have them jump up over the handle and land on the other side on their feet *(SEE FIGURE 59)*. All players should learn how to build up their jumping muscles, but mostly "Centers", and "Power Forwards", need to work on this drill.

Practice:
You can start with 5 year olds by raising the handle to about 8 inches off the floor, through 12 year olds at about 12 inches off the floor. They should start

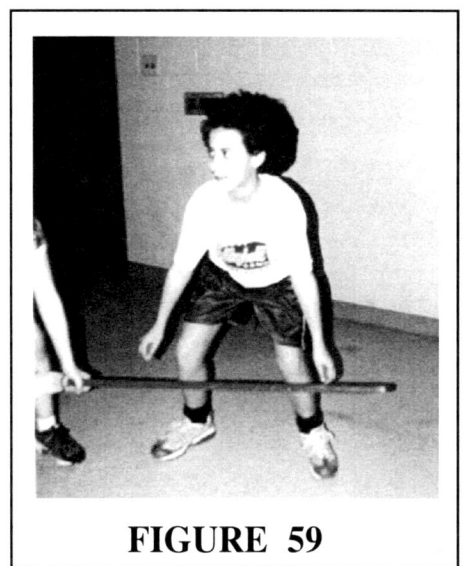

FIGURE 59

out by doing about 5 of these each day. You can increase the number of repetitions, and raise the handle higher and higher as they get a little stronger, and better at doing it. A *TIP* here is, have them swing their arms down and bend their knees a little just before jumping up.

Drill No. 33- Grab the Flag

The Basics are:

This jumping way up, and reaching, drill will help them improve on their jumping straight up ability as well as their reach for rebounds ability. It will also help centers get up in the air higher, to block shots. The idea is, make it into a habit for them to jump up, and not stand flat footed on the floor. All players should learn how to jump up, and reach, but mostly "Centers", and "Power Forwards", need to really work hard on this drill.

Practice:

Take the same broom , an old rag (Flag), and stick the rag into the bristles, just enough to hold it in place. Then you hold the broom, and the flag, way up in the air. Have your son or daughter stand directly underneath the flag, then jump straight up, and try to grab it first with one hand, then with two hands. Watch how far their feet get up off the floor, then once they get up high enough to grab it, then keep raising the flag just a little bit, out of there reach, so they have to keep getting up higher to grab it *(SEE FIGURE 60)*. They should start out by doing 5 of these with <u>each</u> hand, then you can increase the number a little as they get stronger, and better at getting higher off the floor. A *TIP* here is, have them push off with their left foot when just the right hand goes up, and push off with the right foot when just the left hand goes up.

FIGURE 60

Drills for Shooting

Shooting is probably the second most important skill after footwork, in playing basketball. Shooting is throwing, or should I say pushing, the ball at the basket to score points. If no one shoots, there is no score in the game to determine the outcome. Shooting is an art form. Watching a good shooter is like watching ballet. It is a skill you can learn with a lot of practice, and learning the fundamental moves. Improving on their mechanics increases their confidence. The thing to remember for the little kids is, it takes the arms and the legs to get the ball up to the basket. The age of the player will determine how much, of each one, will be needed. 5 and 6 year olds are going to need both, just to get the ball up to the basket. Teach them to shoot the ball with one hand, not two hands. 5 and 6 year olds will also have to lower the ball almost down to below their knees, and use a lot of leg push, just to get it up to the basket.

Practicing using the correct form is training the muscles to respond almost automatically. When you start teaching a 5 year old all of this, he is probably going to be pretty good at it by the age of 12 years old. However after a few years and a lot of teaching, then if your son or daughter just is not learning, or having any fun, then maybe they need to take up another sport like soccer, where they use mostly their feet. Some of our best basketball coaches say, there are four things that make a great shooter.

- *The correct mechanics and techniques.*
    Kids need to constantly work on their fundamentals because this is what developes muscle memory reflexes.

- *A good mental approach.*
    Kids have to understand, and concentrate on, using the correct techniques. Set goals, then work hard on reaching those goals.

- *Many hours of practicing.*
    Just knowing the correct techniques is not going to help kids, without many hours of practicing.

- *Being accountable.*
    Kids need to learn to be accountable for each shot they take. Take high percentage shots only, not shots they can't make. Teach them to keep track of how many they make, and how many they miss.

Drill No. 34- Holding the Ball

The Basics are:
 The very first thing to teach your son or daughter is how to hold the ball. The second thing to explain to them is, control the ball with their finger tips. There is more than one way to hold the ball, but there is one way that is more effective, especially for the younger kids. First have them put the ball in the palm of their strong hand (usually the right). It should rest on the pads of the hand between the thumb and the fingers, and with some space between the palm and the ball. Then support, and steady, the ball with the other hand *(SEE FIGURE 61)*. Next have them grip the seams, with the fingertips of the pushing hand. The fingers that propel the ball are the "index", and "middle", fingers. These two fingers should be in the center of the ball. Coaches have found a good way to accomplish this. And that is, place these two fingers around the valve *(SEE FIGURE 62)*. All players need to work on this drill.

FIGURE 61

Practice:
 To practice this drill, you will need to find a court, or at least a flat driveway to work on. Have your son or daughter stand out in front of you about 6 feet away. Then you, mom or dad, take the ball and toss it to them. What they have to do is catch it, spin it around, with the non shooting hand until the valve is centered in the fingers. Once they have done that, they just pass the ball back to you. Keep doing this, over and over until they get in the habit of doing this automatically.

Drill No. 35- Shooting Stance

The Basics are:
 When your son or daughter gets ready to shoot the ball, they should have their feet

FIGURE 62

and shoulders squared up (Facing) to the basket. Sometimes in the game it's hard to get squared up to the basket. When practicing though they should always try to do this. The foot, on the side of the shooting hand , should be just a little bit out in front of the other foot. The ball should be held just above, or below the knee, for the 5 and 6 year olds. It can be up higher, around the waist or chest, for the bigger kids. It kind of depends on the arm strength the shooter has *(SEE FIGURE 63)*. For left handers, this stance is going to be reversed or just the opposite. All players need to work on this drill.

FIGURE 63

Practice:

To practice this drill, mom or dad, have your son or daughter take the ball, and go out to the free throw line. Have them relax. Then say "GO", and have them get into the stance correctly. Stand under the basket, watch them, and check their form. Make any necessary corrections. Have them stand there and just relax again. Then say "GO", and have them get into the stance again. Keep doing this over and over until they get in the habit of doing this automatically.

Drill No. 36- Body Mechanics

The Basics are:

The head should remain still, all the way through the shot until the ball goes in, or hits the basket. The eyes need to stay on the target. For a target, have them focus on the center of the square on the back board. The eyes should stay focused on the target, all the way through the shot until the ball goes in, or hits the basket. The arm, and the ball, should not block your vision as you focus on the basket *(SEE FIGURE 64)*. They need to be positioned, so they can see the basket with both eyes. A little jump up on the shot is ok, but not forward. The body *should not* drift, or sway from side to side, or fall back during the shot. This will all throw off their balance, and cause the shot to be out of line with the basket. Less body motion during the shot will give you a better chance of making it. The back foot, on the side opposite the shooting hand, should be pointed at

RIGHT   WRONG
FIGURE 64

45 degrees outward on *free throws*, to help the player stay in balance better when starting the shot *(SEE FIGURE 65)*. But this is only on free throws. It won't work on moving shots. On moving shots, they should land in the same place with their feet that they jumped from, or maybe just a little bit forward of that spot. All players need to work on this drill.

Practice:

To practice these techniques, have them go back to the free throw line as in the previous drill. Then you, mom or dad, get under the basket and watch their form. Say "GO", and have them get into the shooting stance *(SEE FIGURE 63)*. Next have them slowly take a jump shot, and check all of their body mechanics as they make the shot. Make any necessary corrections, and have them keep executing shots. Practice makes perfect.

Drill No. 37- Shooting Mechanics

The Basics are:

It takes the arms and legs both to propel the ball to the basket. One great pro player nicknamed the "Rifleman" made the comparison of shooting a a rifle, and shooting a basketball. He said, "Think of your feet as the butt of the rifle, your arm as the barrel, and the hand is the front of the barrel". Everything between the feet, and the hand, must move in a fluid motion toward the target . Teach 5 and 6 year olds to shoot with one hand, not two, right from the start. They need

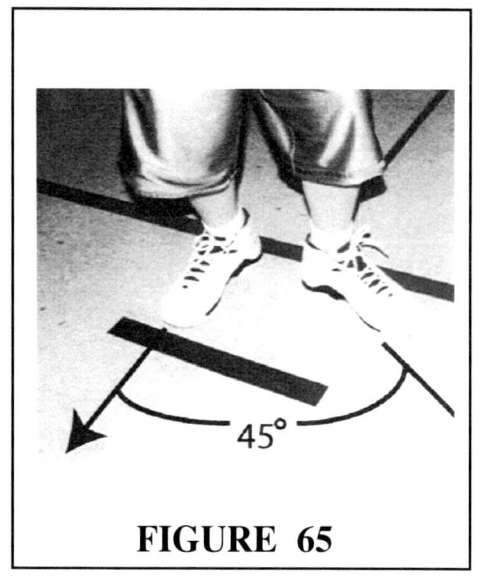

FIGURE 65

C B A
FIGURE 66

to bring the ball down to below their knee, on still or non moving shots *(SEE FIGURE 66-A)*. Teach them to bend at the knees *(SEE FIGURE 66-B)*, then snap up with a big push *(SEE FIGURE 66-C)*. As they get older they won't have to rely on the legs, and the lower hand position as much.

On moving shots, they have to scoop the ball up off the dribble, with the shooting hand, get the proper grip, then jump stop *(SEE FIGURE 58)*. Next they push up with both feet, set or cock the ball *(SEE FIGURE 67)*, then make the shot. At the set position, the shooting arm should be shaped like the letter "L". With the upper arm parallel to the floor. The wrist on the shooting hand should be bent back, or cocked *(SEE FIGURE 68)*, ready to make the push for the shot. All players need to work on this drill.

Practice:

Practice these techniques the same way as in "Drill No. 36, except stand first directly behind them, and then in front of them, to make sure you can see that they are following the shooting and body mechanics correctly. On free throw shots, make sure they are keeping the back foot turned outward *(SEE FIGURE 65)*. Also make sure they stay balanced while shooting. First have them make some free throw shots.

FIGURE 67

FIGURE 68

After they have tried some free throw shots, have them dribble up to the free throw line and make some jump shots. What they have to do in this case is, dribble really low, scoop the ball up by rolling the shooting hand around underneath, and explode into the "jump stop" *(SEE FIGURE 58)*. Next they push up hard, set the ball with their hands *(SEE FIGURE 67)*, and make the shot. Also see the Jump Shot, Drill No. 40.

Drill No. 38- Release, Follow Through, and Arc

The Basics are:

The release, follow through, and arc, on the ball are very important, in finishing the shot. For the release, the ball should be placed just above the eye on the shooting hand side, and moved just to the outside enough to still be able to see the basket *(SEE FIGURE 69)*. The elbow on the shooting hand needs to pointed at, and aligned with the basket *(SEE FIGURE 70)*. The wrist should snap forward, with the "index", and "middle", finger rolling off the ball, and causing it to back spin a lot.

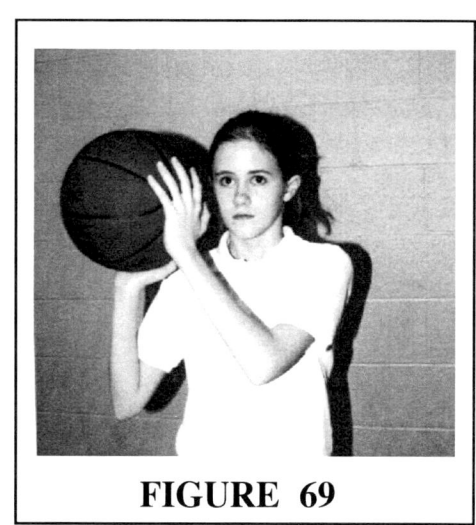

FIGURE 69

FIGURE 70

These two fingers should be the last to touch the ball as it rolls off, and that is where the good spin is generated. The push has to be upward, and not forward. On the follow through, after the ball has been released, the wrist is bent over forward forming what has been called "a gooseneck" *(SEE FIGURE 71)*. Also on the follow through, keep your eyes focused on the target all the way to the basket. Another little aid to the shot is, imagine you are grabbing the front rim with the shooting hand, just after you release the ball. To get just the right arc on the shot, sometimes takes lots of trial and error evaluation. Too hard a push, and too much arc, and the ball will hit way up on the back board. Too little arc, and the ball may fall short of the basket. All players need to work on this drill.

Practice:

There are two good drills now being used a lot, to help them develop a good release and follow through. They are the "lie on your back drill", and the "sit on the chair drill".

FIGURE 71

Sit on the chair Drill

Take a chair out to driveway or court free throw line, or a little closer for 5 amd 6 year olds. Have your son or daughter sit in it, and face the basket. Have them take the ball and shoot it in the basket, using the correct release and follow through technique *(SEE FIGURE 72)*. This will help them build up their arm strength, learn how to put the correct arc on the ball, and how to line up their elbow correctly. Have them do at least 5 to 10 of these every day, or more if they have time. Have them do this drill first with their strong hand, and then their weak hand.

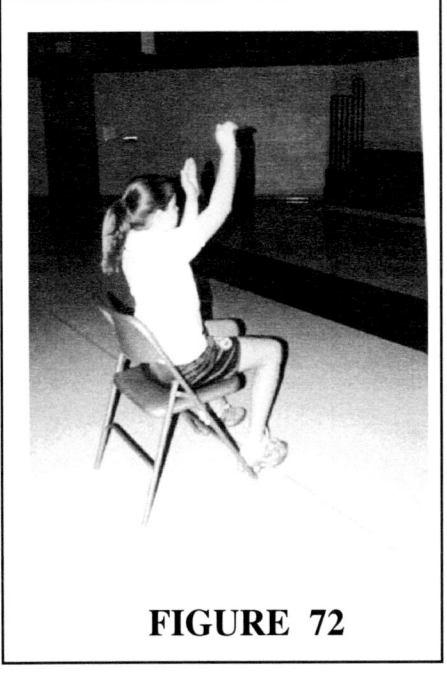

FIGURE 72

The lie on your back drill

Have your son or daughter go out to the court or back yard grass, take the basketball, and lie on their back. Their legs should be spread apart a little bit, then they take the ball in the shooting hand. Support it with the other hand, hold it above their chin and to the side a little bit *(SEE FIGURE 73-A)*. Next have them push the ball straight up hard, so it comes right back down to their hand, without having to move it *(SEE FIGURE 73-B)*. Just as the ball leaves their hand, have them hold the "goose neck" position *(SEE FIGURE 71)*til the ball starts to come down. They make the catch, then push it right back up again. As they

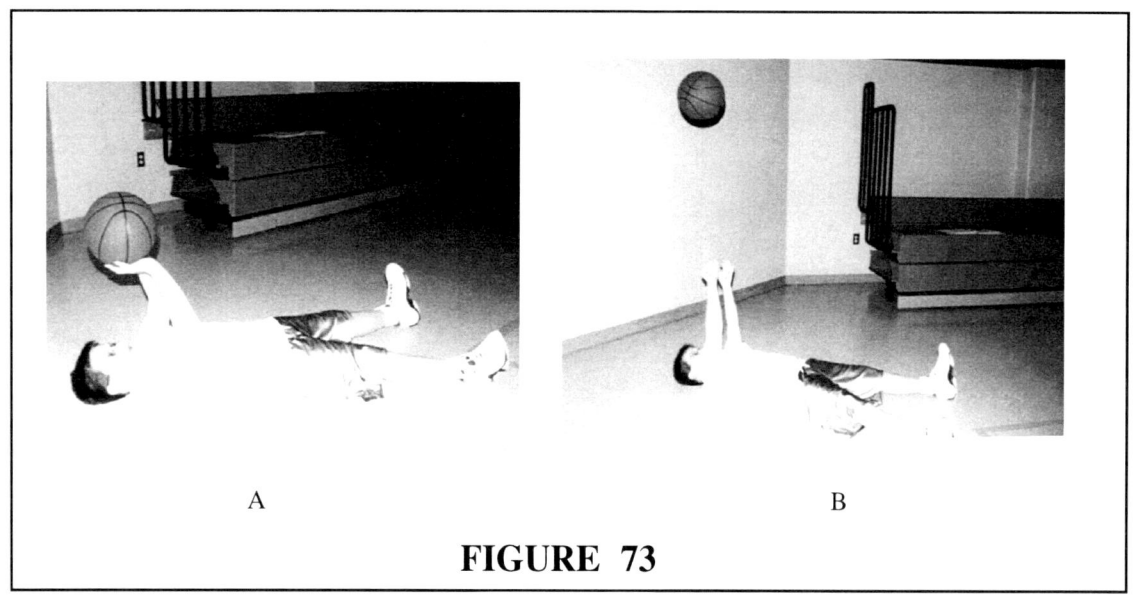

FIGURE 73

get better at doing this, have them try to push it up higher and higher. The seams of the ball should be parallel to the floor before they push it up. Teach them to rotate the ball around with the non shooting hand until the fingers on the shooting hand are across the seams. Have them do this "push the ball up" drill, first with their strong hand, then their weak hand.

There is a little game you can play with them. When they push the ball up, and it comes straight back down into their hand, it counts as a basket. If it doesn't, it counts as a missed shot. Have them remember how many they made, and how many they missed.

Some coaches have come up with a way to check if your release and follow through are correct, or if they have flaws. What they do is take a 3/4 or 1 inch wide strip of white tape, wrap it around the center of the

FIGURE 74

basketball, and perpendicular to the seams *(SEE FIGURE 74)*. Then they have the player stand at the free throw line and make a jump shot. By standing behind them, they look to see if the ball apears to be wobbling as goes up to the basket. If it does appear to be wobbling, then the player has a flaw in their release, follow through, or grip. If the ball is rotating symetrically, it will not appear to be wobbling, and their technique is ok.

Drill No. 39- Lay-up Shots

The Basics are:

The lay-up is the easiest, and the first, shot to teach your son or daughter. A lay-up shot is taken within 6 or 8 feet of the basket. It can be taken from the right, or the left, side of the basket. For the little kids, "side lay-ups" should always be ***banked*** in off the back board. This is because it has a higher percentage chance of going in the basket. If you aim directly for basket, it has the possibility of hitting the rim, on the way up or the way down, and bouncing back away from the basket. When you come in from the right side of the basket, you push off with the left foot, then raise and lift their right foot ***(SEE FIGURE 75)***. When you come in from the left side of the basket, you push off with the right foot, then raise and lift your left foot. Just as you come in from the right side of the basket, and your left plant foot is forward, and when you are about to jump up, you bring the ball around near your right hip area using two hands. The right hand should be almost on top of the ball, and the left hand around on the left middle side of the ball ***(SEE FIGURE 53-A)***. Coming in from the left side everything would be just the opposite ***(SEE FIGURE 53-B)***.

FIGURE 75

When you go into your jump from the right side, shift the shoulders to the right a little bit, to protect the ball from the defender. Then as you are into your jump, you bring the ball all the way up to head heigth with both hands, using your left hand to protect and shield the ball around to your right side until the last minute release. Make the release at the highest point of the jump. Then you push release the ball, aiming about at the center of the square on the back board. Never watch the ball, always focus and keep your eyes on the target (the center of the square). The <u>more back spin</u> you put on the ball as it rolls off your fingers, the <u>more downward</u> the bounce off the back board is. That what gives the ball a better chance of directly going into the basket, instead of bouncing off the rim.

Coming in from the front lay-ups are now called "power lay-ups". However, I suggest the little kids come in from the side because it is a higher percentage shot for them. At least until they get to be 12 years old, or older. The reason is, the little 5 to 7 year olds don't always have enough arm or jump strength, to push it up with enough arc to get it over the rim. When they do get big enough to try a "power lay-up", they do every thing the same as from the side. Except they aim, and focus, on a spot just over the top of the basket as they come straight in. Also they softly push the ball up, without the spin and wrist snap.

Practice:

Start out by having them stand under, and to the right side of the basket, then go through the shot in <u>slow motion</u> with their right hand. Point out to them to step forward, push off with the left foot, raise and lift their right foot, pull the ball in ***(SEE FIGURE 53)***, bring it up to head heigth ***(SEE FIGURE 76)***, then extend their right arm toward the basket ***(SEE FIGURE 75).*** Then have them go under and to the left side of the basket, and repeat the same action with their left hand. In this case they would step forward, push off with their right foot, raise and lift their left foot, pull the ball in, bring it up to head heigth, then extend their left arm. If you start out by teaching them both sides of the basket, it will make them a better shooter. Now after they have been through all of this, in slow motion, you can get into the moving part of the drill. That is, they can practice how to come into the basket, and what kind of <u>reads</u> they need to learn. Reads on defender position are what they need to look for, and observe as they approach the basket.

<u>DRIBBLING IN FROM THE RIGHT SIDE</u>

Have them start by going out to the mid court line, or out by the side walk in your driveway (when you have a basket above your garage door). Next have them dribble towards the basket, dribbling the ball with their right hand. When they get within 6 or so feet of the basket, they make a jump stop, push off, jump up and **bank** the ball into the basket, aiming at the approximate center of the square painted above and behind the basket on the back board. Make sure they push the ball up with some wrist spin. After they have done this a few times, then either place a folding chair or stand

FIGURE 76

yourself under the basket, and just a little to the right side. This is to simulate a defender in position to block the shot. At this point they have two choices. They can go ahead and move around the defender, to the right side, a little bit and **bank** the ball in. Or they can fake going to the right with their head and eyes, then go around the defender and underneath to the left side of the basket, and make a reverse lay-up.

On the reverse lay-up, there is two basic ways to get the ball into the basket. The most common way is to keep dribbling with the right hand, then just as they get under and just past the basket, then they jump up and use a twisting motion to **Bank,** backward spin, the ball into the basket. This is done by twisting the wrist to the left, which puts a reverse spin on the

FIGURE 77

ball, and causes it to hit the back board and bounce right into the basket *(SEE FIGURE 77)*. The other way is, just after you head fake the defender, you switch the ball over to a left handed dribble, go under the basket to the left side, jump up and **hook Bank** the ball in with your left hand *(SEE FIGURE 78)*.

FIGURE 78

Their *READ* on this shot should be if you <u>do not</u> see a defender in place, in front of you, just go in fast jump up and bank it in. If you <u>do see</u> a defender in place, or out of the corner of your eye you see him coming in parallel and just ahead of you, you have to make the decision of whether you can beat him to the basket. Or you will have to fake him out, and do a reverse lay-up. The decision may also depend on who the defender is. If you see it is a center, or someone taller than you, you will probably have to fake him, or he will come over the top of you and stuff or block the shot. If it is a smaller guard, you can probably out jump him, and bank it in.

DRIBBLING IN FROM THE LEFT SIDE

FIGURE 79

Have them start by going to the mid court line, or out by the side walk in your driveway (when you have a basket above your garage door). Next have them dribble towards the basket, dribbling the ball with their left hand. When they get within 6 or so feet of the basket, they make a jump stop, push off, jump up and *bank* the ball into the basket, aiming at the approximate center of the square painted above and behind the basket on the back board *(SEE FIGURE 78)*. Make sure they push the ball up with some wrist spin. After they have done this a few times, then either place a folding chair or stand yourself under the basket, and just a little to the left side. This is to simulate a defender in position to block the shot. At this point they have two choices. They can go ahead and move around the defender, to the left side, a little bit and *bank* the ball in. Or they can fake going to the left with their head and eyes, then go around the defender and underneath to the right side of the basket, and make a reverse lay-up.

On the reverse lay-up, there is two basic ways to get the ball into the basket. The most common way is to keep dribbling with the left hand, then just as they get under and just past the basket, they jump up and use a twisting motion to *Bank,* backward spin, the ball into the basket. This is done by twisting the wrist to the left, which puts a reverse spin on the ball, and causes it to hit the back board and bounce right into the basket *(SEE FIGURE 79)*. The other way is just after you head fake the defender, you switch the ball over to a right handed dribble, go under the basket to the right side, jump up and *hook Bank* the ball in with your right hand *(SEE FIGURE 80-C)*. All of this is just the reverse, or flip flop, of how you do it from the right side. The *READ* on this shot should just the same as coming in from the right side.

Drill No. 40- Jump Shots

The Basics are:

The next most used shot to teach your son or daughter is the jump shot.

Young kids should be shooting for baskets within a distance of 8 to 10 feet of the basket, especially 5 year olds. They are just not strong enough, at 5 to 7 years old, to shoot from farther out than this range. So, what does this mean. It means that within this range of the basket, they should be learning to take jump shots. For the basic mechanics of the jump shot **See Drill No. 37 and 38.**

Practice:

See the practice for Drill No. 37. To practice this shot have them do at least about 10 or 15 each day, first with the right hand then the left. Also they should move around the basket in a semicircle, and at different distances to take these shots, within the 8 to 10 feet range. Observe their form and mechanics, to make sure they learn this shot well. Not that centers and power forwards don't have to learn this shot, but the young players that really need to work on this shot constantly are "guards", and "small forwards".

The *Tip* here is, you can tell if 5 to 10 year olds are shooting this shot too far away from the basket, by watching their mechanics as they try to shoot. Look for any of these four reasons, to move closer to the basket and make the shot properly. 1.) They bring the ball way down to their side below their knee, with both hands, instead of up by their chin. 2.) Their body has to twist, to push the shot up towards the basket. 3.) They may emit a little grunting sound as they push the ball up because they don't have the strength to get the ball up to the basket, from where they are standing. 4.) The ball consistently does not make it to the basket and falls short.

Drill No. 41- Free Throw Shots

The Basics are:

The free throw is a very special, and important shot. Imagine it as a free shot, without anyone guarding you, or rushing you, to make the shot. And this is why you must teach them to make this shot, and that is just because it is free. Another reason this is important is because you are getting this free shot because an opposing player has fouled you. And if the opposing player gets too many fouls, they are out of the game. To make a free throw, they have to stand 15 feet away from the basket on the free throw line. Both feet should be just back of the edge of the free throw line, and the front or lead foot should be right at the center of the line, pointed straight ahead *(SEE FIGURE 65)*. On the newer hard wood floors, there is a nail right on the center of the line. Start 5 through 10 year olds out about 6 to 10 feet away from the basket, and work their way out as they get better. Have them take a deep breath and let it out slowly to make sure they are relaxed, and not nervous before they start the shot. Lets talk about the knees again here. The knees are what make this shot, its where your power up to the basket comes from. So, make sure they do the drills to make their legs strong. Again, have them imagine *Grabbing* the rim, right after they release the ball. See Drill No. 34 through 38 to go over all of the basics. All players need to work on this shot constantly, it's very important.

Practice:
See the practice for Drill No. 37. They should practice making this shot as much as possible. At least 20 or 30 shots a day, from 6 to 15 feet away from the basket. When they get bored after school, or on the weekend, have them go out to the driveway and shoot free throws. And when they come in ask them how many they made, in a row, without missing (To get them into thinking this way). The *TIP* here is, always make sure you are relaxed before the shot, and always follow through correctly.

Drill No. 42- Tip In Shots

The Basics are:
Tip in shots are very important because if you miss the shot you can still go in and follow your shot to the basket for a tip in, just in case it doesn't go in. This must be a lost art because I never see any young kids practicing this shot. What you have to teach your son or daughter to do is, time the jump up by watching the ball, and learning how to recognize when it is going to miss. And also which direction it is going in after missing. Learning how to do this will only come from a lot of repetitions of this drill. When they see it is going to miss, they need to jump way up high, use their fingers, and a snap of the wrist, to push it off the backboard before it comes down, and into the basket. Or they can use their palm, and fingers, to roll it over the rim and into the basket *(SEE FIGURE 78)*. All players can benefit from this drill, but it is a must for "centers", and "power forwards", who spend most of the time under, and around, the basket.

Practice:
To practice this shot, you will have to start out by having them stand right under and, to the *RIGHT* of, the basket. Then position themselves ready to jump way up in the air. Then you, mom or dad, get on the other side of the basket and

throw the ball up, so that it misses the basket in different ways. Sometimes make it miss by banking it off the back board, and sometimes make it miss by hitting and bouncing off the rim. Have them practice this, from under the *LEFT* side of the basket also. Once they learn how to time their jumps, then they can practice this drill all by themselves. They can do this by stepping back about 8 feet from the basket, then dribbling the ball twice, then shooting the ball at the basket. Next they follow their shot in for the jump up tip in. This is where the leg strength drills come in handy. They should do at least 15 or 20 of these, from each side of the basket, every day if possible. The *TIP* here is, learning to time their jump just right so that their hand is going up just as the ball is falling away from the basket.

Drill No. 43- Hook Shots

The Basics are:

The hook shot is a very special shot because it was designed to make shots in an area of about a 8 foot arc out from the basket. This is another shot I don't see kids practicing these days. If you are "one on one" guarded, in this arc area around the basket, this is a pretty easy shot to make once you learn the technique. The reason being is, you can keep your body and non shooting arm between the shooting arm and the defender. If you can spread the defense out away from the basket, then with some practice, even young kids can learn how to make this shot, which is hard to block. This is a shot that tall, long armed, "centers", or

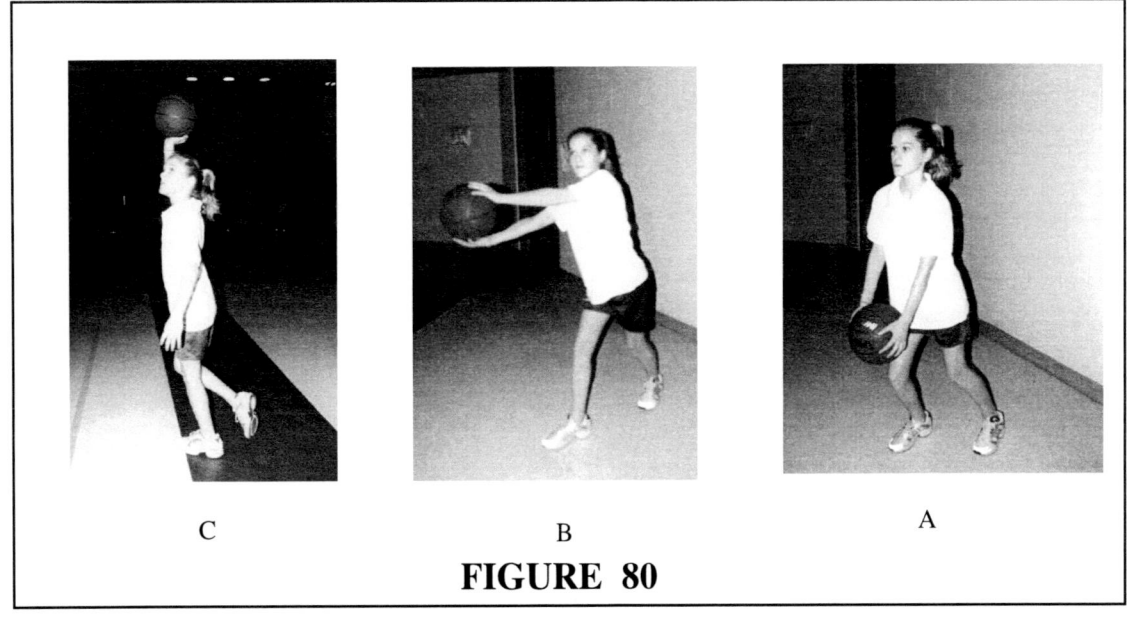

FIGURE 80

"power forwards", should learn how to make. Start by having them stand about 6 or 8 feet out from the basket, with their back to the basket. To make the shot from the RIGHT side of the basket, take the ball in both hands *(SEE FIGURE 80-A)*, fake by turning your head to the right. Then step sideways with the left foot. Next pivot on the left foot, then crossover step to the left with the right foot. Then bring the ball up to about chest high, and extend both hands out. Now rotate the ball around so your left hand is on the upper left top of the ball, and your right hand is underneath the ball *(SEE FIGURE 80-B)*. Next grip the ball tightly in your right hand, let go of the ball with the left hand, and lift swing the right arm over your head and left shoulder, towards the basket. The left arm should be swung around out of the way to the left, close to the body, with the forearm bent in an "L" shape, and forearm parallel to the floor. This is to block the opponent from reaching in. While swinging the arm, look back over the left shoulder, using the center of the square on the backboard as a target. The ball is released off the spread finger tips. Keep looking at the target, all the way through the release and follow through. A little jump up is made by pushing up with the left leg, and lifting the right leg *(SEE FIGURE 80-C)*. To make the shot going to the left of the basket, everything is flip floped, or reversed. This drill is a must for "centers", and "power forwards", who spend most of their time under, and around, the basket.

Practice:

To practice this, start out by having the 5 and 6 year olds stand still with the ball, about 6 feet out from the basket, with their back to the basket. For 7 year olds and up, they can move out to an 8 foot arc distance. I suggest starting out in slow motion, and going through each step. Next have them turn to their left, face their left SHOULDER towards the basket, step to the left, crossover step, then grab the ball with the right hand and support it with the left. Extend both hands out about chest heigth. Then they look back, and shoot the ball up over their head, with a swinging motion. The bicep part of their arm should be ending near their right ear *(SEE FIGURE 80-C)*. This will take some practice for 5 to 8 year olds, to catch on how to makethis shot because their hands are very small in comparison to the ball. If you think you have a center, or a power forward, and you start teaching them how to make this shot when they are 5 years old, they will probably be very good at it by the time they reach 12 years old. After they learn how to make this shot, with the right hand, then switch around and reverse everything, so they learn to make the shot with the left hand.

Once they have learned to make the shot in slow motion, then the next step is to have them dribble the ball twice while moving, right or left in the 8 foot arc area. Then push off with the left leg, jump up, lift the right leg, and take the shot with the right hand. They should learn how to do this with both hands. After they have mastered going to the right of the basket, then have them work on going the other way to the left of the basket. They should practice this shot at least 10 times, with each hand, every day if possible (The more repetitions the better). The *TIP* here is, have them perfect their grip on the ball *(SEE FIGURE 62)*, then work on controlling and supporting the ball while making the arm swing.

Drill No. 44 - Three Point Perimeter Shots

The Basics are:

This shot, out at the 3 point line, may be too much for a 5 year old to practice. However, 11 and 12 year olds should be working on this shot, especially if they are guards, or small forwards. The other shots are worth one or two points, so if you are behind in the game, a few three point shots can help you catch up or get ahead fast. If your younger 5 through 10 year olds can reach the basket from the three point circle, without struggling, then let them work on this shot. However, if they are not even close to reaching the basket with their shot, then don't waste time with them working on this shot. The reason being, they will develop some bad habits trying to reach the basket. And those bad habits might effect their mechanics, on the rest of their shots. Wait until they get older. This is really just a long jump shot *(SEE FIGURE 67)*, way out at the 3 point line. The big difference is you have to push up harder, and get more arc on the ball. The only way to develop this shot is lots of trial and error practice, to get the range of the basket. Your target should probably be a spot right over the top of the ring. The *TIP* here is, watch the target and *not* the ball, all the way to the basket.

Practice:

To practice this shot, have them start out about 10 to 15 feet from the basket, then have them move out farther as their mechanics gets better. They will need strong legs to make this shot. Its all done with the knees, and the push off. Have them use the same basic mechanics as the jump shot *(SEE DRILL NO. 37 & 38)*, except they bend their knees a little more, and snap up harder with their legs. Also have them practice this shot from different spots around the arc, so they get the feel of looking at the basket from different angles. 5 through

9 year olds should do only about 2 or 3 of these shots, from 5 different places around the arc. Kids 10 through 12 years old can do 5 or 6 of these shots, from 5 different places around the arc. Something to point out to you here is, don't put too much pressure on your son or daughter to learn to make the three point shot. The reason is, the shot is hard to make, and the game can be won in many other ways. A good defense causing turnovers, and players making the other regular shots, will work just as well. The *TIP* here is, build up their leg strength so they can reach the basket, and teach them to put a high arc on their shot mechanics.

Drills for Guarding

Learning the different ways to guard an opposing player is a very important part of the defensive game. If an offensive player is allowed to go up the court unguarded, they will probably make a basket. Really it's defense that win games. And defense is guarding. I think the trick in guarding a player is stay real close to them, but go out of the way not to touch them. And the way to learn how to do this is, lots of practice, over and over, with supervision. Several things to remember are, always raise both hands straight up when the player has stopped, and it looks like they are going to pass the ball . And don't look into the opposing players eyes because it makes it easier for them to fake you as to which direction they are going to go. If you teach your son or daughter to look at the players stomach while they are dribbling, they will not be faked out as easily. The other thing to remember is, have them always keep their body between the opposing player and the basket. The following drills are all designed to help give them the skills needed to guard a player.

Drill No. 45- Defensive Stance

The Basics are:
This stance gets you ready for whatever the opponent might do. U.C.L.A.'s great coach, John Wooden, constantly stressed this stance for his players. Many coaches like this stance because it allows the defender to cover a larger area very quickly. One foot is forward, but it doesn't really matter which one. Except when an opponent is being guarded along the "baseline", or "sideline". In that case, the forward foot must be the foot closest to the line. This is to cut off the side lines as a possible driving lane to the basket. The other foot is back. Your weight needs to be evenly distributed on the balls of your feet. The body is bent

at the waist, with the knees flexed and loose. The forward hand is raised and extended toward the opponent. This is to distract them, and block their vision. The other hand is at waist level, ready to block the passing lane on that side *(SEE FIGURE 81)*.

If the opponent starts to dribble around your right side, you pivot off your left foot, and take a long step back with the right foot, right along the path of where the opponent will be making his drive. The right hand reaches out to cut off the dribble or a possible pass *(SEE FIGURE 82-A)*.

If the opponent starts to dribble around your left side, you pivot off your right foot, and

FIGURE 81

take a long step back with the left foot, right along the path of where the opponent will be making his drive. The left hand reaches, and swings out to cut off the dribble or a possible pass *(SEE FIGURE 82-B)*. All players need to work on this drill, to improve on their defense.

Practice:

To practice this have them go out to the court, or driveway, and get into their defensive stance *(SEE FIGURE 81)*. Then you, mom or dad, get about 6 feet in front of them, with a basketball, and slowly start to dribble right at them. When you are about 3 feet away, them make a sudden break, and try to dribble around them to the right. What your son or daughter has to do is, quickly pivot off their left foot, turn to the right, and take a long step back with the right foot. As they do this, they have to reach out with their right hand,

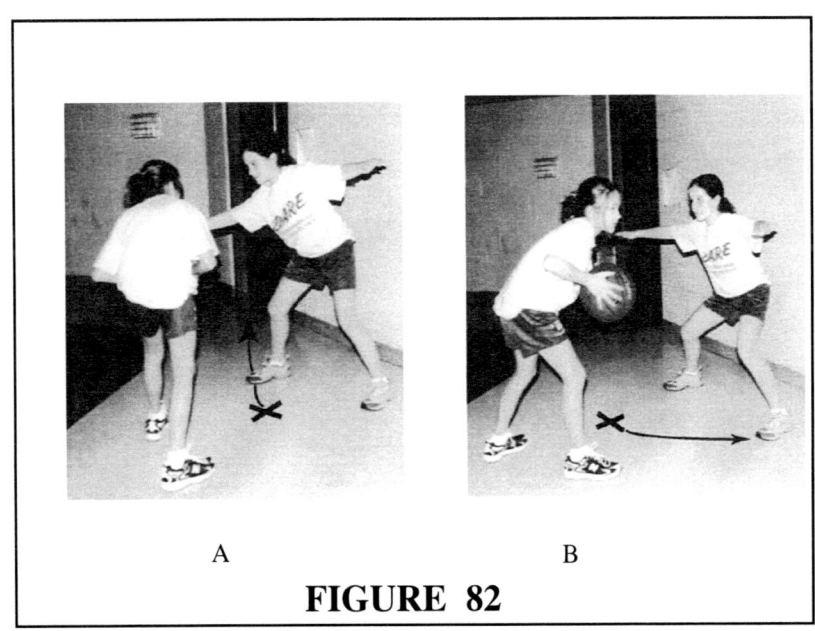

FIGURE 82

down low and block your dribble path. When they do block your path, be carefull, and don't hurt them by running hard into them. Remember, this is practice. Just stop when they have effectively blocked your path. After doing this several times, around their right side, then switch and try to go around the leftside. While doing all of this, mom or dad, try to watch and see if they are pivoting, and stepping off the correct foot.

Drill No. 46- Shuffle Slide Side Step

The Basics are:

When you are backing up the court, and guarding a player as they come up the court, make sure to stay low and slide sideways when they try to go around you. While maintaining a position in front of them, you should get into a "ready position". Your feet should be shoulder width apart, knees bent, hands outstretched in front of you with palms up, and elbows slightly bent **(SEE FIGURE 52).** Make sure that you teach them to never cross over step with their feet if they have to move sideways, slide shuffle sideways instead, to stay in front of the player they are guarding. This is where this drill comes in if they are "guards", or "small forwards". It is to get them used to sliding sideways.

Practice:

To practice this have them go out to the court, or driveway, or even in the back yard, and get into their defensive stance (ready position). Then you, mom or dad, stand in front of them and move sideways as if dribbling the ball **(SEE FIGURE 84).** They have to shuffle slide sideways all the way across the court, or driveway, to one side then all the way back across to the other side. They have to do this while staying directly in front of you. "Guards" should do this drill every day for at least 10 minutes. The *TIP* here is, stay low with the knees always bent and with the back straight up.

FIGURE 84

Drill No. 47- Boxing Out

The Basics are:

This drill is for "centers" and "power forwards". They play mostly in the low post, next to the basket. What you have to teach them to do is, play right in back of the opposing center, or power forward. While in that position they can put their hand on the back of the player, but don't lean on them, or restrict them from moving *(SEE FIGURE 85)*. This is where strength comes in. The center and power forward have to be fast enough to get back down the court on defense, and get into their defensive position. They use the strength of their feet, and lower body, to not let the opposing player back up, or push them toward the basket.

FIGURE 83

"Boxing out" is when the opposing player turns, and makes a shot over your hands stretched straight up, then you whirl around quickly and put your back to them. Then you put both arms out to the side to keep the opponent from getting around you *(SEE FIGURE 83)*. This keeps them from going to the basket for any possible rebound. Sometimes this is called "blocking out".

Practice:

To practice this drill, have your son or daughter go out about 5 feet in front of the basket, and to the right side. Then get into a defensive "ready position" *(SEE FIGURE 52)*. Then you, mom or dad, get in front of them with a basketball, and turn so your back is facing the basket. Make sure they put their hand on your back, then you pivot, turn, and try to shoot a basket over the top of them, or around them. When they see that you are going to turn and try to shoot, they have to stay right with you, outstretch their hands straight up, and try to keep you from getting a good shot *(SEE FIGURE 86)*. Next, right after they see the ball leave your hand, they need to whirl around and put their hands out to their sides, face the basket, and block you

FIGURE 85

FIGURE 86

from getting around them to get any rebounds *(SEE FIGURE 83)*. Then if the ball does not go in the basket, they have to jump up for the rebound. You should practice this with them for at least 10 to 15 minutes at a time, and from different spots in an arc around the basket. The *TIP* here is, have them stay just close enough to the opposing player, so they don't foul them. And if the opposing player wants to run into your son or daughter, then have them keep their hands up without fouling, lean back, hold their position, and let the opposing player take a charging foul into them. And explain to them that when they see the player is going to shoot then always have them get at least one, if not two hands, way up high in front of the opposing player to distract them.

Defensive Drills

Team defense is probably the most important part of the game. Its defense that wins games. What this means is, stopping the opposing team from scoring points. Each member of the team has a particular job to do when the offense sets up in a certain way. What the offense is doing tells the defense how to set up to defend. "Guards" have a certain way to play, when the opposing team brings the ball in. "Forwards" go to a certain position on the court, when an opposing player is out on the wings, or at the top of the key. "Centers" go to a low post, or a high post, depending on what type of defense their coach wants to play. The basic defenses that are used are the "Man to man", and the "Zone". In the case of "Man to Man", each player has a particular player to guard, which he stays right on top of, or next to, most of the time.

When a "Zone" defense is played, each player has a particular area of the court to guard, no matter who comes into that area. And some coaches like to use a combination of these defenses in certain cases. We will show you how and what fundamentals to teach at each position.

Drill No. 48- Man to Man point Guard

The Basics are:

When a point guard is playing "Man to Man", there are several

responsibilities they have on defense:
1.) Don't let the player you are guarding beat you to the basket on the dribble. Stay right Between him and the basket at all times.
2.) Always force the player you are guarding, to the outside of the court. Don't let him dribble to the middle of the court.
3.) Don't let the player you are guarding shoot a three pointer, without getting your hands up in front of them to distract them, but don't foul them.

The reason the point guard has these responsibilities is, the opposing guard which they usually guard, will be doing these same kind of things when they come up the court in an attempt to score.

Practice:
To practice this play you, mom or dad, get a basketball and go out to the mid court line, or out to the sidewalk in front of the garage driveway. Then first try to dribble up the middle right to the basket, then your son or daughter has to get into their defensive stance *(SEE FIGURE 52)*. Next they try to get in front of you in such a way as to force you to go to the outside of the court, or driveway, and away from the basket. If they do manage to get in front of you as you go to the basket, be careful not to knock them down, especially if you are out on the driveway. This is because they will probably get hurt, or skinned up, if they go down on the asphalt. When they accomplish this technique, then go back and do it again, over and over. You should work on this with them at least 10 or 15 minutes at a time. The <u>*TIP*</u> here is, they must have quick feet in sliding in either direction. And only watch your opponents stomach and not his eyes, when they start to move. This way you won't get your feet tangled up, and get faked out by the opponent, when they change directions.

Drill No. 49- Man to Man Shooting (Off) Guard

The Basics are:
When the shooting guard, or "Off Guard" as they are called, are guarding the other opposing guard without the ball, they have the responsibility of staying right in front of them. This is so they can't catch a pass from the ball handling guard. What they will have to learn how to do is, keep watching the player they are guarding, and out of the corner of their eyes watch the player bringing the ball up the court. This is important for the younger kids because the opponent will pass the ball wildly sometimes without looking, and this lets the off guard intercept the pass.

FIGURE 87

Practice:

To practice this play, you will probably need to find another boy or girl about the same size as your son or daughter, to help you out. Then you, mom or dad, take the basketball and go out to mid court, or out to the sidewalk in front of your garage. Then have your son or daughter go to a spot about 5 feet in front of the basket, and get into their ready stance *(SEE FIGURE 52)*. Then have your helper kid get right behind them. Next you start to dribble the ball towards them, and have the helper kid sneak around them on either side. When the helper gets into the clear, you try to pass them the ball while your son or daughter tries to knock down or catch the pass. Work with them on this for at least 10 or 15 minutes each day, or on the weekend. This will teach them to learn how to stay in front of the opposing player, and not let them catch the pass *(SEE FIGURE 87)*. The *TIP* here is, have quick feet in sliding left or right to stay with the helper kid.

Drill No. 50- Man to Man Guards Rotating

The Basics are:

This drill is for either "point", or "shooting", guards learning to rotate to help out. I might point out here that for young kids, just starting out at the Atom or Bantam division level, the coaches may not want them to play rotation yet. However, I think your young son or daughter still needs to know what rotation is, and how it works. Rotating is when a player is guarding an opposing player, man to man, and they leave that player to help out one of their team mates guard an opponent driving in for a shot. This is kind of complicated for little kids because it is a team concept where one of their other team mates has to leave the player they are guarding, and pick up the player you were guarding . It takes a while for a young team to learn this.

Practice:

To practice this play, you will need to find another kid about the same size as your son or daughter, to help you out. Then you, mom or dad, take the basketball and go out to mid court, or at the sidewalk in front of your garage. Then have your son or daughter, and helper, go to a spot about 5 feet in front of the basket. Next your son or daughter gets in front of the helper, and gets into their defensive "ready stance" *(SEE FIGURE 52)*. Then you, mom or dad, start dribbling the ball slowly towards the basket. Have the helper move slowly to their left, with your son or daughter sliding and following them. When they have moved far enough out the way, to the right of the basket, giving you an open lane to the basket, then you break and dribble fast towards the basket. Try to make a lay-up shot. What your son or daughter has to do is keep their eye on you, and when they see you start to drive to the basket, they break away from the helper, and slide back to their right. This is to get in front of you, so you can't make the shot. This is also called "switching off", by some coaches. There is not much room in your driveway, so you might have to walk through this slowly at first until they see how it is done. Then switch, and have them and the helper move to their right (your left), so they get a feel for working on this from the other side of the basket. They should practice this for at least 10 to 15 minutes at a time, if possible. The *TIP* here is, have them learn how to watch you out of the corner of their eye, and break away just as you start to speed up and drive to the basket. This will take some practicing, but don't give up on them because they can learn how to do it. And, mom or dad, remember you are bigger than they are, so don't run over them and hurt them on the way to the basket.

Drill No. 51- Man to Man Guards Converge

The Basics are:
This is a stop the ball handler drill. When the opposing guard brings the ball in, and starts to dribble faster up court, both guards suddenly break fast and converge in front of them. Next they get as close as they can without fouling (Touching), put their hands up, wave, and keep the opponent from passing the ball. Usually this will result in a mistake by the ball handler, and causes a turnover (Your team grabs the loose ball). This drill is mostly for "guards", but it won't hurt if "small forwards" learn this also.

Practice:
To practice this play you, mom or dad, take the ball and go out to mid court, or the sidewalk, in front of your garage. You will probably need a helper kid, about the same size as your son or daughter, to help you on this drill. Have your

FIGURE 88

son or daughter, and the helper, go to a spot about 5 feet in front of the basket, and spread out about 10 feet apart. Then you start dribbling the ball fast towards the basket. When your son or daughter, and the helper, see you start to dribble fast, they both quickly break and converge on a spot right in front of you. They both get their hands up while you stop and pretend to pass *(SEE FIGURE 88)*. Since you are more than likely going to be a lot taller than they are, they probably won't be able to smother you like they would a kid their own size. But they can still get the practice in, on what to do. And they can still try to knock the ball down when you attempt to pass it. They should practice this at least 10 to 15 minutes at a time if possible. If they are making mistakes then stop and correct them. The TIP here is, quick feet and learning how to break quick enough, to allow them time to get in front of the ball handler to cut them off.

Drill No. 52- Man to Man Small Forward

The Basics are:

The "small forwards" job, in the man to man defense, is a little more simpler than a guard. They have to basically keep passes from getting in to the low post player they are guarding. If the small forward lets the ball handler pass the ball, in to the player they are guarding in the low post area, he probably will score a basket most of the time. Also they need to seal off the player they are guarding, from dribble driving the basket. They have to learn how to steal any passes to the player they are guarding when that player attempts to cut around in back of them for a lay-up.

Practice:

To practice this play you, mom or dad, take the ball and go to the mid court line, or out to the sidewalk in front of your garage. You will need another kid, about the same size as your son or daughter, to help you out. Send your son or daughter to a spot way out on the wing area, to the right side of the basket. Have the helper kid get in front of them, then you start to dribble towards the helper, then have the helper cut around to their left, behind your son or daughter, towards the basket. Then you attempt to pass them the ball. Your son or daughter then has to whirl around to their left, raise their right hand, slide step, then stay between the helper and you. Then your son or daughter has to look back at you, and attempt to knock down the pass, or catch the ball (**SEE FIGURE 89**).

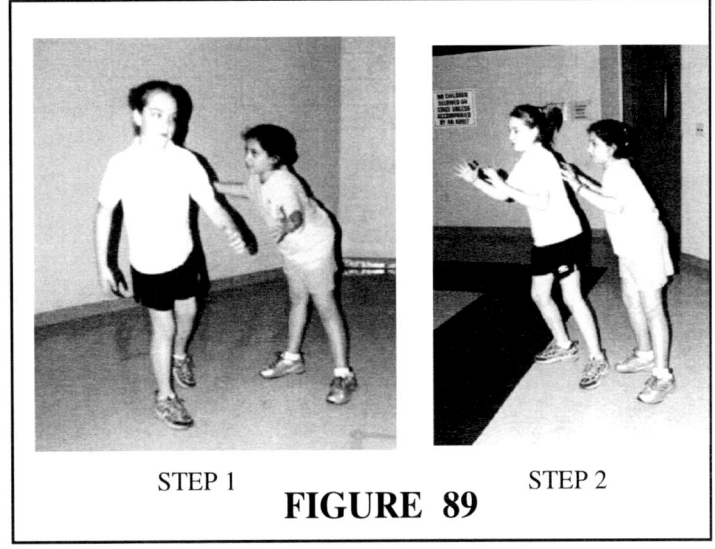

STEP 1　　**FIGURE 89**　　STEP 2

To make this play work for them, they will have to learn to keep quickly turning their head back and forth to watch you, then watch the helper.

If the player they are guarding does get the pass, and takes a short jump shot, then your son or daughter has to remember to whirl around, and box them out from getting to any rebound (**SEE FIGURE 83**). After you practice this over on the right side, then move over to the left side and flip flop or reverse everything. They need to learn how to make this play, on either the left or right wing area of the court. They should practice this at least 10 or 15 minutes at a time, if possible. If they are making mistakes, like on whirling, then stop and correct their mistakes by walking them through this slowly. The *TIP* here is, quick feet, and the cross over foot whirl. This is why doing all that practice with the crossover foot agility drill comes in handy. If they whirl the wrong way they will sometimes get their feet tangled up, trip, and fall down. Leaving the player they were guarding wide open to go to the basket for a lay-up.

Drill No. 53- Man to Man Power Forward

The Basics are:

The" power forwards" job, in the man to man defense, is also a little more simpler than a guards responsibilities. They have to basically keep passes from getting in to the low post player they are guarding. If the power forward lets the ball handler pass the ball in to the player they are guarding, in the low post area, they probably will score a basket most of the time. When they are in the low post area, they need to seal off opposing players attempting to drive to

FIGURE 90

the basket. They have to learn how to steal, or knock down, passes to players attempting to cut around, or behind, them for a lay-up. And if you get right in front of, and between the player and the basket, just let him run into you and take a charging foul. If you are bigger than the player cutting to the basket, this should not be a problem. Just use your strength, to hold your seal off position.

Practice:

To practice this play, you mom or dad, take the ball and go to the mid court line or out to the sidewalk in front of your garage. You will need another kid, about the same size as your son or daughter, to help you out. Send your son or daughter to a spot about 5 feet out from the basket, and to the right side. Have the helper kid get in front of them, then you start to dribble, then have the helper cut around to the left, and behind, your son or daughter, towards the basket. Then you attempt to pass them the ball. Your son or daughter then has to whirl around to their left, raise their right hand, slide step, then stay between the helper and you. Then your son or daughter has to look back at you, and attempt to knock down the pass, or catch the ball *(SEE FIGURE 89)*. To make this play work for them, they will have to learn to keep quickly turning their head, back and forth to watch you, then watch the helper. Sometimes pass the ball to the helper, then have your son or daughter slide in front of the helper, attempting to drive to the basket, seal them off, and take a "charging foul" *(SEE FIGURE 90)*. To get the foul called though, remember to explain to them that they have to be in position already directly in front of the player breaking for the basket, and between that player and the basket.

If the player they are guarding does manage to get the pass, and takes a short jump shot, then remember to teach them to whirl around, and box the player out from getting to any rebound *(SEE FIGURE 83)*. After you practice this over on the RIGHT side, then move over to the LEFT side and practice, by flip floping and reversing the moves. They need to learn how to make this play, on either the left or right, at the low post area of the court. They should practice this at least 15 or 20 minutes at a time, if possible. If they are making mistakes, like on whirling, then stop and correct their mistakcs by walking them through this slowly. The *TIP* here is, quick feet, and the cross over foot whirl. This is where doing all that practice with the crossover foot agility drill comes in handy. If they whirl the wrong way, they will sometimes get their feet tangled up, trip, and fall down. This leaves the player they were guarding wide open, to go to the basket for a lay-up.

Drill No. 54- Man to Man Center

The Basics are:

The main job of the center is, stop opposing players from driving to the basket for lay-ups, box out after they shoot, and grab all rebounds. They are usually the tallest, and the biggest, player on the court. But because they are so tall and big, they are not always to coordinated. So they have to work hard to learn all the basic fundamentals. Here are the basics they need to learn:

1.) After a player releases their shot, they have to whirl around and box out.

2.) When they are guarding, or going out to try and block an opposing players shot, they need to get both arms straight up to obstruct that players view of the basket, or to block the shot.

3.) They have to learn to not react to an opposing players faking with the ball.

4.) They need to learn to keep their hand lightly on the opposing centers back, but not lean up against him, and get a foul called against them.

5. They have to learn to anticipate where the player they are guarding wants to go, then when that player starts their move, your son or daughter needs to beat them to that spot.

6.) Don't play in front of the player they are guarding because the ball handler may make a lob pass over their head, and let that player make a basket.

7. They have to learn how to block shots, by getting a hand on the ball and deflecting it. Also along with this, they need to learn to not touch the players arms or body, but just the ball.

Practice:

To practice these plays, have your son or daughter go out to a spot about 5 feet in front of the basket. Then you, mom or dad, take the basketball and go out to spot about 8 feet in front of them. Next start your dribble right to the basket, and try to make a lay-up shot. Their job is, come out, and get right in front of you and block your path to the basket, and take a charging foul if you run into them *(SEE FIGURE 90).* You may want to practice this in slow motion, so no

FIGURE 91

one gets hurt accidentally. Work on this play about 3 or 4 times.

Then on the next time, stop short of dribbling just in front of them, jump up and try to shoot a short jump shot. Their reaction should be to come right in front of you when they see you are going to shoot, instead of dribbling by them. They should jump up with both hands straight up in air, in front of your view of the basket *(SEE FIGURE 91)*. Work on this play 3 or 4 times.

Now they are not sure when you are going to change again, so then you dribble right at them. Then when you get close to them, give them a head fake, try to sneak around them on the other side, away from the fake side. Do this for about 3 or 4 times.

For this next practice exercise, you will need a helper kid, to help you. Have your son or daughter stay in the same starting place, then put the helper behind them under the basket. Then you start your dribble right at them, but when you start to get close, you lob the ball over their head to the helper. This has to done quickly before your son or daughter can get their hands up. After a few times, they will see when you are going to lob the ball, then they should stop, jump up with one or both hands straight up in the air, and try to catch the lob. Do this 3 or 4 times.

On this practice exercise, both of you go back to the same places, start your dribble right at them, and tell them they have to try to block the shot this time. Then start your dribble, and when they come up to block your path, stop and try to make a short jump shot. Since they are practicing the block, have them watch the ball and nothing else when they come up to make the block *(SEE FIGURE 92)*. Observe and make sure they get one or both hands on the ball, and not hit you or your arm for a foul. And since you are probably much taller than they are, make it fair and don't jump up for the shot. Do this for about 3 or 4 times.

FIGURE 92

For this practice exercise, have them go to their starting spot again. Then you, mom or dad, get right in front of them, with your back to them. This is a another type of drill for shot blocking. Then when you are ready, whirl around to either side of them, and try to shoot a jump shot. What they should do is put their hand lightly on your back, to keep their space, until they see what you are going to do *(SEE FIGURE 85)*. When they see that you are going to whirl around to the side of them, they drop their hand on your back, then slide over to the same side you turn to. Next they put their hands up, to make it harder for you to see the basket, or they try to block the shot *(SEE FIGURE 91)*. Make sure they don't touch you or your arm for a foul. If they touch the ball though, its ok. All they need to do is touch enough of the ball to deflect it, not try to slap it way into the next county. Do this for about 3 or 4 times.

For this practice exercise, both of you take the same positions as before with you right in front of them, with your back to them. This is a drill for "boxing out" and rebounding. Then when you are ready, whirl around to either side, and make a jump shot to the basket. Their reaction should be to try to block your view or the shot *(SEE FIGURE 91)*. If you do manage to get the shot off on its way to the basket, their reaction should be to whirl around and box you out from trying to go to the basket, to grab the rebound *(SEE FIGURE 83)*. The *TIP* here for all these drills is, do a lot of work with your son or daughter on the coordination drills, so they develop quick feet.

Drill No. 54- Man to Man Screens

The Basics are:
This drill is for all players, but mostly for guards and forwards. Screens are when a player is guarding the opponent, they are assigned to guard, and that player uses one of his own team mates as a blocker. This is to get rid of your son or daughter guarding them, so they can get open for a pass or a shot. What happens is the ball handler maneuvers around, so his team mate (usually a big center or power forward) can slid in between the two of you. Then they stand there flat footed and still. Then just when the blocker gets between you, the player breaks in another direction, then they move to an open spot to catch a pass, or get a jump shot off to the basket. Of course when you try to slide with them, you run into this big player blocking you, from staying with the player you are guarding. The defensive player being screened (your son or daughter) has two choices. They can try to go around the blocker, and stay with their man, or they can yell "SWITCH", and stay guarding the blocker. Wwhen they yell switch, one of their nearby team mates picks up and guards the opposing player, who

FIGURE 93

slipped around the screen. The danger with the switch is, if you are a small guard, you may end up trying to guard a bigger player, who may get the ball then over power you to the basket for a shot. Also this concept will only work if the players on your son or daughters team have been taught how to "SWITCH" correctly. If they have *not* been taught, your son or daughter will have to keep practicing on how to get around the screen, then it is a must that they maintain contact with the player they were guarding.

Practice:

What you can do to practice this play is, teach them both ways. And they will have to learn to analyze the situation, to determine which technique to use if they are *"Screened"*. First you, mom or dad, take the ball and go out to mid court, or out to the sidewalk in front of the garage. At this point you will need a helper, who will act as the blocker. Have your son or daughter go to a spot about 5 feet out in front of the basket. Have the helper get just to their left, and next to them. Then you start your dribble right at your son or daughter. When you start to get close to them, you *fake* going around to the left side of them. Next the helper will have to get right up close to them, and when the helper can see that you are getting close, they just stop. Then you switch and go around to the right of them, for a lay-up to the basket. And at that point the helper has to get right off their left front shoulder, and stay in contact with them to act as a blocker between you and your son or daughter *(SEE FIGURE 93)*. At that point have them yell "SWITCH", and move around quickly in front of the blocker and start guarding them. And just for your information, when the blocker does this for the ball handler, it is called a "Pick and Roll" play. The "Roll" comes from having the blocker roll back towards the basket after the switch, then the ball handler passes back to him for the lay up. Work on this play for at least 4 or 5 times every practice until they are beginning to get the idea of how it feels when they get blocked. Remember to explain to your son or daughter that if at all possible, be ready for the screen and fight through it, to stay with the player they are guarding. They only do a switch when they see that there is no way they can get around the screen.

For the next practice exercise you, and your son or daughter, go back to the same starting positions, except this time the helper stands to the right side of them. All of you do the same things as before, except this time when you make your change of direction to the left, the blocker just stands there leaving room for your son or daughter to go around behind them (to let then make a play on you). Your son or daughter then goes right around behind them, and keeps sliding to their right, guarding you from getting to the basket for the lay-up. Do this play about 4 or 5 times every practice. The *TIP* here is, work on their quick footwork and learning how to tell when to fight through the screen, or stay there for the switch and guard.

Drill No. 56- General Shot Blocking

The Basics are:

All players need to learn the basics of shot blocking on defense. However, the two players that need to really work on learning this technique are "centers", and "power forwards". This is because they are usually the tallest players on the team, and they have the longest arms. To get the blocked shot called fair though, the ball has to be on the way *up* to the basket, and *not* after it starts back down on its trajectory. If they swat (block) it on its trajectory down to the basket, its ruled as "goal tending", the basket then counts. So, the best way to make a block is, get your hand on it just as the ball handler starts the shot, or the pass *(SEE FIGURE 92)*. At this point explain to your son or daughter that in order to practice the shot block they need to focus in on the ball, as they get close to the ball handler, then never take their eyes off the ball. To learn how to do this will just take a lot of practice, over and over. If you can teach them to make blocks, they will go far in basketball, especially if they are big and tall

Practice:

To practice these techniques, have your son or daughter go to a spot out about 5 feet in front of the basket. Next you, mom or dad, get about 10 feet out in front of them, so you have space to dribble the ball. Dribble straight at them, and first try to stop just in front of them, and shoot a short jump shot *(SEE FIGURE 67)*. What they should do is, come right up close to you and focus on the ball. Then just as the ball bounces down and starts to come up,

FIGURE 94

FIGURE 95

they reach out, focus on the ball with their eyes, then with the palm of their hand facing forward, push it right at the ball *(SEE FIGURE 94),* deflecting it away. Do at least about 5 or 6 of these plays at every practice.

If they are not catching on how to do this, then you might try this out to quicken their hands. Stand right in front of them, hold the ball tightly in front of your chest *(SEE FIGURE 95).* Then have them stand about 2 or 3 feet in front of you. Hold tight on the ball and holler "Reach". When they hear that, they lunge out with their hand and hit the ball as fast as they can, with the palm facing forward and fingers up. They need to bring the hand back quickly though so they don't foul the opponent. Then react to whether they made the block or not.

The other way to attempt to make a block is, watch the ball handlers free hand. Then when they get close to you, the free hand will move around to grab the ball to steady it for a pass or a shot, then have your son or daughter quickly switch their focus to the ball, and reach for the block *(SEE FIGURE 95).* Do at least about 5 or 6 of these plays at every practice. The *TIP* here is, teach them to have quick hands, focus, keep their eyes on the ball, and don't look at <u>opponents eyes</u> when they get close, all of this as they are about to make their reach.

Drill No. 57- Making Steals

The Basics are:

All players need to learn the basic fundamentals of making steals. But mostly "guards" and "small forwards" need to learn this technique. All of the following are qualified as a steal:

1.) Grabbing the ball away from an opposing player, without fouling them.
2.) Making a "Held ball" play, and causing the ball to go over to your team on a possession.
3.) Intercepting an opposing players pass, and gaining control of the ball.
4.) Batting the ball off an opposing player, who is standing in bounds, and having it go out of bounds, giving your team the possession.
5.) Batting the ball off an opposing player, and having it deflected to a player on your team.

Practice:

To practice making steals, first have your son or daughter go to a spot out about 12 feet in front of the basket. Then you, mom or dad, will need to get a helper. Have the helper stand about 5 or 6 feet behind them. Then you, mom or dad, go out to mid court or out on the sidewalk in front of the garage. Then slowly start to dribble right at your son or daughter. After a couple of dribbles, attempt to pass the ball to the helper. Explain to the helper that they have to start out right behind your son or daughter, then they can move to either side while your son or daughter watches you. When they are clear to the either side, then you stop, and pass the ball to the helper. Your son or daughter has to watch you and the helper, by looking back and forth, and when you pass the ball they attempt to catch it. Do this about 4 or 5 times each practice.

For the second practice, you stand about 6 feet in front of your son or daughter, and slowly start to dribble the ball towards them. When you get close, give them a head fake, start dribbling faster, and try to go around either side of them. And when you get close, they need to start focusing on the ball, and attempt to grab it away from you. And they have to accomplish the steal without touching you for a foul. This is very hard to learn, without fouling the opponent. They will only learn this by practicing it, over and over. Do this at least about 4 or 5 times each practice.

For the third practice, both of you go back to the starting position. Start dribbling the ball right towards them, then just like the second drill, make your move to go around them. Except this time have your son or daughter just grab the ball with both hands, and hold on for a *"Held Ball"*. Their move should be to just watch the ball when you get close, then grab it and hold on. Make sure to keep dribbling, but let them grab it some of the time. Do this at least 4 or 5 times each practice.

For the fourth practice, have your son or daughter stand right near a base line or a side line. Pick a spot where there is room for them to jump up in the air out of bounds. Then you, mom or dad, take the ball and stand about 3 or 4 feet away from them. Next you lob the ball up in the air, just slightly out of bounds. Have them jump up in the air, out of bounds, and swat (bat) the ball while it is still in the air, right back at you. While in the air they need

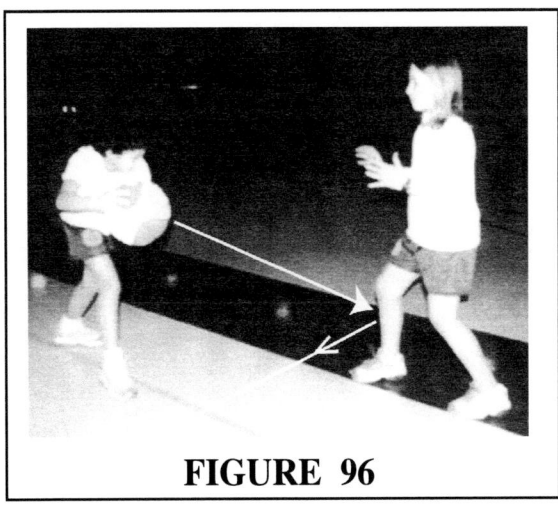

FIGURE 96

FIGURE 97

to take aim at your lower legs, which is where they want to swat the ball *(SEE FIGURE 96)*. The ball should hit your lower legs, then bounce out of bounds. Explain to them that if they swat it up higher, you will be able to catch it, and it won't go out of bounds. They will need to practice this play a lot because it is very hard to learn, especially for 5 to 7 year olds. You may want to wait until they get older, to practice this technique with them. Do this at least about 4 or 5 times each practice.

For the fifth practice, both of you go back to the starting positions on the forth practice. You will need a helper again for this technique. Have the helper go to an inbounds spot about 6 feet away from you, mom or dad. To start the play you, mom or dad, lob the ball up in the air. Except lob it inbounds, slightly away from your son or daughter. What your son or daughter has to do is, jump up as they go out of bounds, and swat (bat) the ball off your legs so that it goes directly to the helper *(SEE FIGURE 97)*. The ball should bounce off your lower legs, down low, where you can't catch it. Something to point out here mom or dad, since you know what they are trying to do, don't reach down and catch it. Just stand there and see where it hits on your legs. This will be very hard for them to learn. If they can't seem to get it to deflect off of you to the helper, don't worry about it. Most of the time the situation where they would need to do this will never come up. However it is a legitimate steal play, and they need to at least know how it works. So make sure they know how to at least attempt it. Do this at least about 5 or 6 times, at maybe two practices, so they will remember. The *TIP* here is, work on their quick hands and feet, and have them work on keeping their eyes only on the ball.

Drill No. 58- Man to Man Rebounding

The Basics are:

All players should learn the techniques of rebounding. But mostly "centers", and "power forwards", need to really work on this technique. This is where those drills on jumping come in handy. They have to get strength in their legs, to be able to get way up in the air for rebounds. Many times your tall son or daughter may not be to athletic, with respect to their jumping abilities. I have watched many young boys and girls, who are centers, just stand flat footed under the basket, and wait for the ball to come down to them. If the coach puts you under the basket on defense, it's probably because he wants you to get most of the rebounds. If your son or daughter has these problems, and plays under the basket, you will have to light a fire under them to make them aggressive.

Teach them to be aware of where the ball might go when a shot is made. To get the rebound they have to be in the right spot, or it might come down on the opposite side of basket from where they are standing. And once they get to the right spot, you need to teach them to "box out" the player they are guarding, or any opposing player in that spot. Teach your son or daughter that rebounding is their job on defense, no matter what position they play. In a "man to man" defense, if all the players keep the opposing player they are guarding from getting a rebound, they have done a good job.

Practice:

To practice rebounding you, mom or dad, take the ball out to a spot about 14 or 15 feet out in front of the basket, or by the sidewalk in front of the garage. You will need a helper to work on this play. Have your son or daughter go out to a spot about 5 feet in front of the basket. Have the helper go to a spot about 4 or 5 feet away from your son or daughter. Then you, mom or dad, shoot the ball at the basket. Try to make your shot miss going in the basket, and bounce off the rim in some way. When they see you make your shot, both your son or daughter and the helper need to turn, face the basket, and attempt to grab the rebound. If your son or daughter can see that the rebound might go towards the helpers area, they need to slide over in front of the helper and "box them out" of position, by getting between them and the basket *(SEE FIGURE 83)*. And point out to your son or daughter that when they "box out", they have to keep pushing backwards, maintaining contact with the player they are boxing out. Also tell them to not be afraid to use their behind (no hands though), to push with , and maintain contact with the opponent.

FIGURE 98

Then when the ball starts to come down, they jump way up in the air to grab it away from the helper

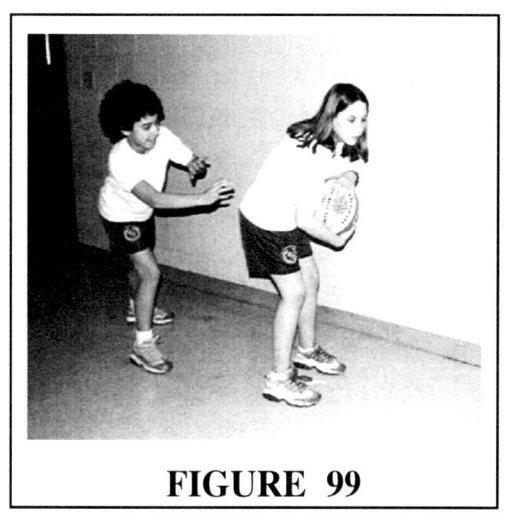

FIGURE 99

(SEE FIGURE 98). When they go up in the air on the left side of the basket, they should reach up with their left hand, and bend the free hand at the elbow, to keep other players away from the ball. And when they go up on the right side of the basket, they should reach up with the right hand. As soon as they make contact with the ball on their finger tips, they need to quickly bring the other hand up, grab the ball with both hands around it, then come back down so that the helper can't reach over and knock the ball loose *(SEE FIGURE 99)*.

Work on this play at least 5 or 6 times each practice. The *TIP* here is, make sure they use their behind to push way back, help them learn how to judge when to jump up, and then make sure they do.

Drill No. 59- General Diving for the Ball (Loose Ball)

The Basics are:

Not every coach wants to teach this skill, but believe me it is an important part of the game. All Players need to learn how to do this. U.C.L.A.'s John Wooden stressed this to his players all the time. What this is mainly for is, learn how to get to loose balls, and gain possession.

Practice:

For practicing this technique, you better go out to the back yard, or the park someplace where there is thick grass. Also if you can afford it, get them some knee pads for this drill, so they don't hurt their knees while practicing. To practice this play you, mom or dad, take the ball and go out about 10 feet in front of them. Have your son or daughter get into their "ready stance" *(SEE FIGURE 52)*. Next you roll

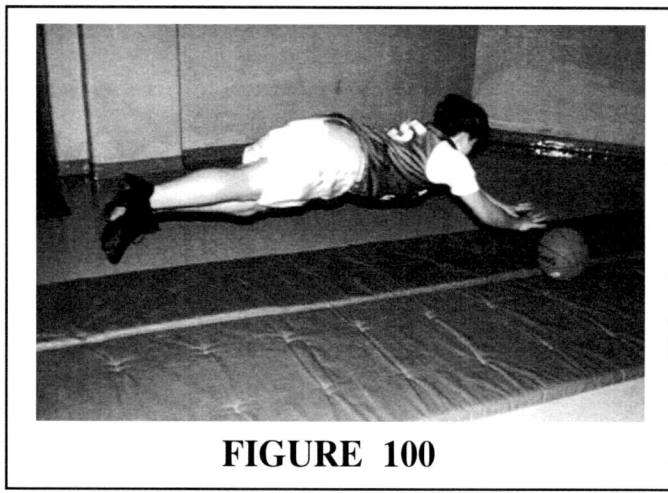

FIGURE 100

the ball slowly, at a spot about 5 feet to the side of them. First to the right of them, then to the left of them. What your son or daughter has to do is, watch the ball with their eyes focused on it, turn, and dive out in the air to intercept the ball *(SEE FIGURE 100)*. Once they do get their hands on the ball, they need to cover it up with both hands so that an opposing player does not come up and grab or knock it away. Teach them to be aware of where the nearest opposing player is. If no opposing player is close, then they can quickly get straight up and to their feet. But if an opposing player is right next to them, they can roll away in the opposite direction, and scramble to their feet.

If they just lay there with the ball, an opposing player can come up and grab onto the ball for a *"Held Ball"*. And that could be a turnover if the possession is in favor of the other team. So once they learn how to get to the ball, work with them on practicing how to get up quickly with the ball. Also if they see that they are going to just barely reach the ball, but not be able to catch or control it, teach them to knock it away out of bounds. Practice this at least 5 times to one side, then 5 times to the other side. The *TIP* here is, use a quick foot slide in the direction of the ball, then a push off and dive, using the lead foot as the push off foot. Also make sure they always keep their eyes on the ball.

Drill No. 60- Guards in a Zone Defense

The Basics are:

In a simple common zone, such as a 2-3 zone, both guards have the responsibility to guard the perimeter wing areas. One guard has an area on one side, from the free throw line out to the wing perimeter on that side. The other guard takes the same area on the opposite side. The problem with this defense is, the opposing team might have 3 good outside shooters. What that does is, it leaves 2 guards that have to guard 3 players from taking an easy jumper, or a 3 point shot. And that usually makes for a big mismatch. In the zone though, if those players do get by the guards and into the lane, they are no longer the responsibility of either guard. The center, or a forward, has to pick them up. When the ball handler is out in the wing area, another player has to slide over and help guard the opposing center, by getting in front of them. This is to keep them from getting a pass from the ball handler. This would be one of the forwards. In this 2-3 zone, the guards also have the responsibility to keep the ball handler from dribbling in between them, to the basket, or making a short jump shot. They have to also stop any one of the 3 players, from penetrating the perimeter. Playing in a zone defense, you should always get your hands up to deflect passes,

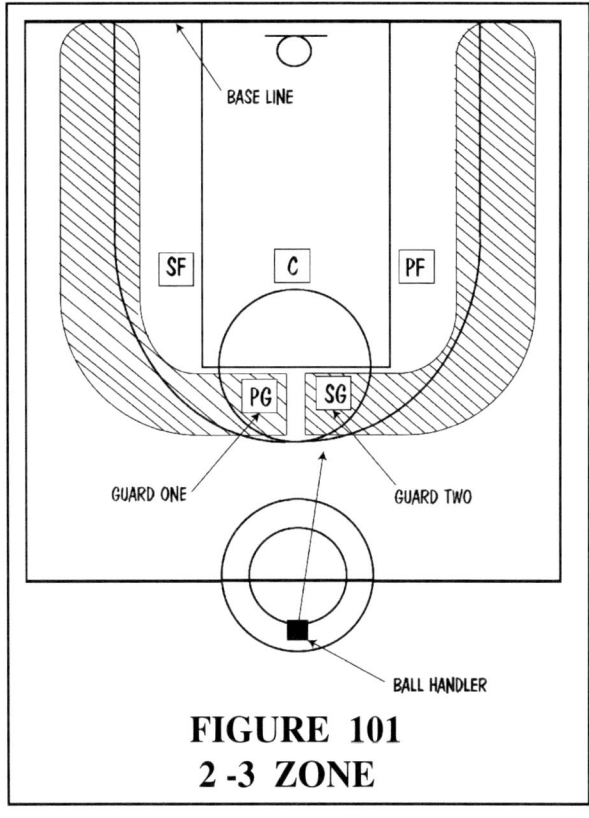

FIGURE 101
2-3 ZONE

from the opposing players because you are not playing real close to them, like in a man to man defense.

Practice:

To practice this play, have your son or daughter go to a spot out about 15 to 18 feet in front of the basket (About at the free throw line) **SEE FIGURE 101.** You will need a helper to work on this play. Then take the ball and you and the helper go out to mid court, or out on the sidewalk in front of the garage. Next you start dribbling the ball right at your son or daughter, and have the helper move right along parallel with you, but on the wing. When you get close to your son or daughter, try to dribble around them. Other times try passing over to the helper, then the helper tries to dribble around them. What you have to teach your son or daughter is, to slide in front of you and block your path. Then the minute you pass over to the helper, they have to rotate (slide) over towards the other part of the court, but within their zone area only. What this teaches them to do is rotate, and follow. Look at the diagram for 2-3 zone defense, and point out to them which basic area they have to defend **(SEE FIGURE 101),** instead of guarding man to man style. What they basically have to learn is to rotate around, and face, the opposing players as they come down court into their zone. I wouldn't practice this too much with the 5 to 7 year old kids. Just enough so they understand how it works. When they get on their first team, then you can see what kind of defense their coach is running. Usually coaches don't try to teach a zone defense until they have been playing a few years. The *TIP* here is as the opposing guards start to get near your son or daughters zone, they need to get their hands up, and rotate slightly towards the side the ball handler is on.

Drill No. 61- Forwards in a Zone Defense

The Basics are:
In the 2-3 zone, the forwards have to guard the wing areas until their guards get up into their locations, then they go back to their own zone area, and guard that side of the basket. What forwards basically do is, kind of form a line with the center, to keep the opposing players from getting through the line and sneaking in behind them, under the basket for an easy shot. They need to make sure that no opposing player gets around them on the base line *(SEE FIGURE 102)*. If they can force the opposing players to go around them, towards the middle of the court, they will get more help there from their team mates. If an opposing player moves right to the base line, they need to guard them very tightly, so they can not catch a pass for an easy basket.

Practice:
To practice this play you will need one or two helpers. Then you, mom or dad, take the ball and go out to mid court, or out on the sidewalk in front of the garage. Next have your son or daughter go to their area on the right side of the basket. Then you start dribbling the ball right at your son or daughter, and the helper moves right along with you, but parallel along the right side of the court. Then suddenly have the helper break for a spot right on the base line, and on the edge of the line for the right side of the lane (The low post area). As your son or daughter sees the helper break for that spot, behind them on the base line, they have to block the helpers path and force them into the lane area in front of them where the center is *(SEE FIGURES 2 & 102)*. While doing all of this, make sure they stay in their zone area. Again practice this a few times with them, to make sure they understand what to do. But don't spend a lot of time on it until they start playing a zone defense on their team. I have

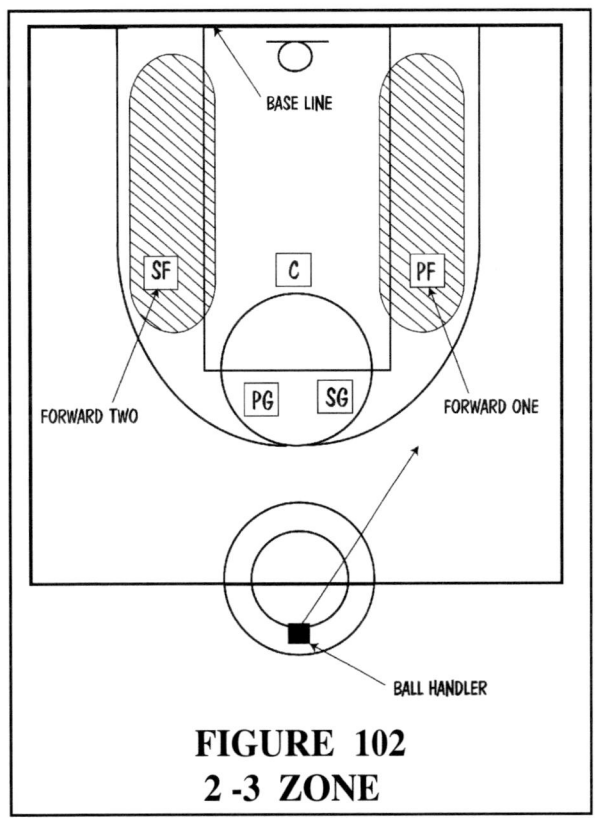

FIGURE 102
2 -3 ZONE

watched some of the young 7 and 8 year old teams play, and I could not tell what defense they were using. If you don't know, don't be afraid to ask the coach, are they playing a zone defense. The *TIP* here is, make sure they get their hands up when an opposing player heads into their zone. And make sure they seal off (Keep them from catching a pass) any opposing players that try to get to, or camp under, the basket in the low post area *(SEE FIGURE 2)*.

Drill No. 62- Centers in a Zone Defense

The Basics are:

In a 2-3 zone, the center has to guard the paint in the center of the lane, and the low post areas on either side of the basket. The center forms kind of a blocking line, with the two forwards. If an opposing player tries to drive to the basket, up the middle of the lane, from the wings or the base line, the center has to seal them off (Keep them from breaking through) **SEE FIGURE 2**. The center also has to seal off any opposing players that break through the forwards, and down the base line. The center always has help around the post area, in a zone defense, with a forward on each side. However, it is still their main job to box out and rebound, if an opposing player does get off a shot at the basket ***(SEE FIGURE 83)***. The area the center needs to defend is really quite small, compared to the area a guard has to cover *(SEE FIGURE 103)*.

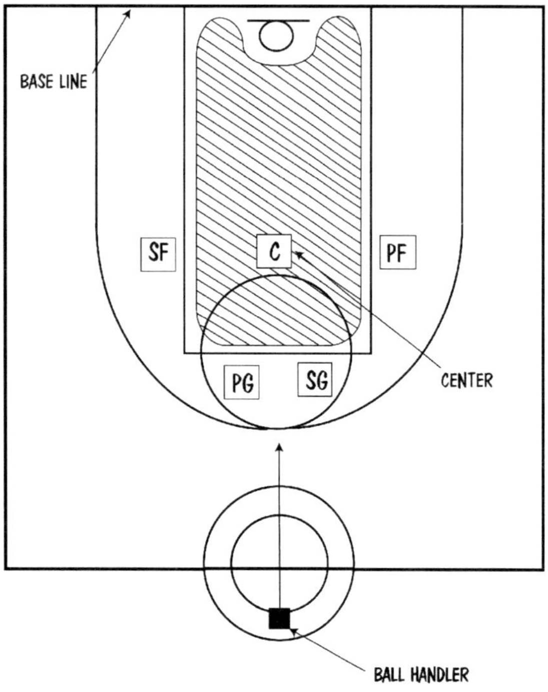

**FIGURE 103
2 -3 ZONE**

Practice:

To practice this play you will need one or two helpers. Then you, mom or dad, go out to mid court, or on the sidewalk in front of the garage. Next have your son or daughter go to their area in front of the basket. Then you start dribbling the ball right at your son or daughter, and the helper moves right along with you, but parallel along the right side of the court. When you get close to your son or daughter, attempt to drive around them right to the basket. The centers job is to get in front of you, and take a ***charging*** *foul* if necessary, but keep you from getting around them for a basket.

Practice this a few times, then the next time you dribble at them, pass the ball to the helper over on the right side, just before you get to your son or daughter. The helper goes way out in the wing area, and on the base line, and waits for your pass *(SEE FIGURE 2)*. When the helper gets your pass, they try to dribble drive right down the base line to the basket. What your son or daughter needs to do is, just as they see you pass the ball way over to the helper, swing around quickly, and move over to the low post area on the right side of the basket. And what they have to do when they get there is, get in position to seal off before the helper can dribble to the basket, for a lay-up shot. Again as I said before work on this play a few times, but don't spend a lot of time on it until your son or daughter gets on a team using a zone defense. The *TIP* here is when they see the opposing team start to come up the court, they get their hands up to deflect any quick passes. And have them work on their quickness of feet, in turning, and pivoting , to move to the seal off spot.

Drill No. 63- Rebounding & Steals in a Zone Defense

The Basics are:
Use the same drills as in the man to man defense section of the book *(SEE DRILLS 57 & 58)*. There is no difference in either man to man, or zone defenses, for improving on these skills.

Practice:
For steals and rebounding in a zone defense, the practice would be the same as in ***DRILLS 57 & 58,*** for "man to man".

Drill No. 64- Other Zone Defenses

The Basics are:
So far we have shown the 2-3 zone defense, mostly because it is one of the more popular zone defenses. However, there are many other zone type defenses. One of the other more popular zone defenses

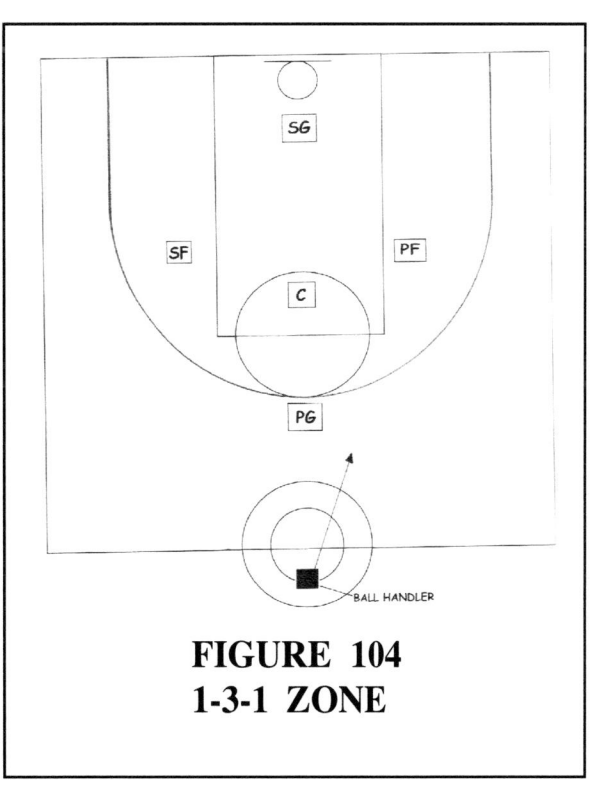

**FIGURE 104
1-3-1 ZONE**

is the 1-3-1 *(SEE FIGURE 104).* This defense is designed to force the opposing team to take long corner shots. It also makes it harder for the opposing team to get rebounds.

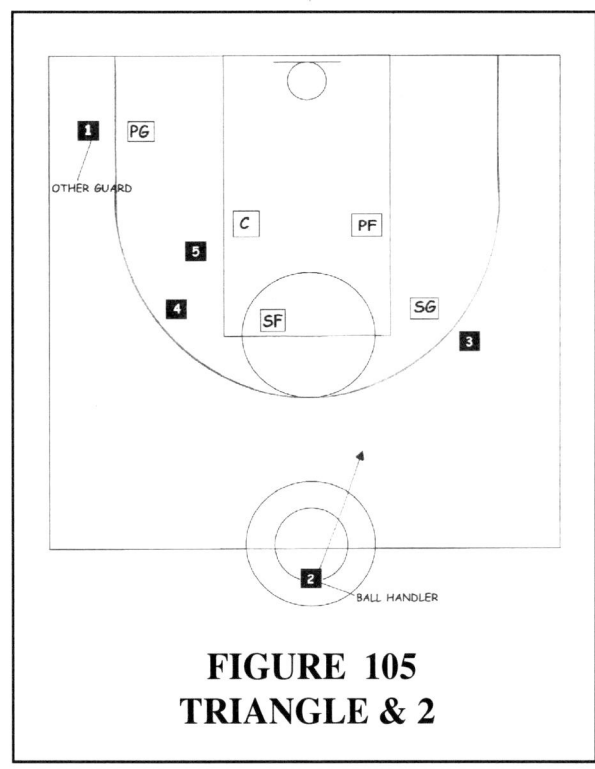

**FIGURE 105
TRIANGLE & 2**

There is a "Triangle and Two" type of zone defense *(SEE FIGURE 105).* This defense is designed to have the three triangle players in the paint *(SEE FIGURE 2),* play a zone defense, and keep any player from penetrating to the basket. The other two players rotate around, play man to man, and keep pressure on the ball handlers. So actually this is a combination defense, not a full zone type defense.

Another defense that is common is the "Box and One". This defense is designed to stop the other team when they have one big dominant, tall, player. The four players in the box play a zone defense. The other player tightly guards the dominant player where ever they go, and keep a constant pressure on them. *(SEE FIGURE 106).* The player, that guards the dominant player, has to have a lot of endurance because they will have to chase that player all over the court, most of the game. And they will have to be a very good defensive player, to stay out of foul trouble. This is also a combination defense. The best defensive guard, or forward on the team, needs to play up in the front of the Box, to also help keep the dominant player from penetrating the Box Zone area

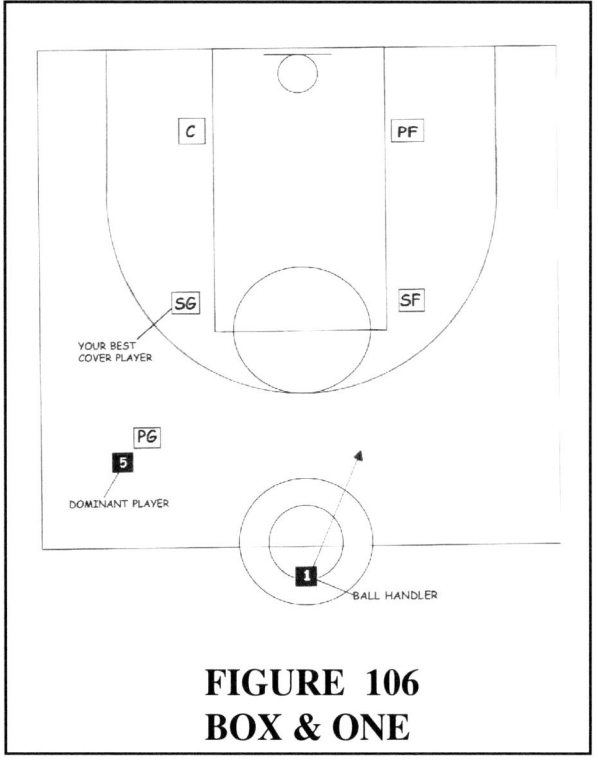

**FIGURE 106
BOX & ONE**

of the paint *(SEE FIGURE 2)*. This strategy could work against a youth team that has maybe only one good, tall, player on their team.

All of these defenses work much in the same way as the *"Man to Man"*, and *"Zone"*, defenses covered in **DRILLS 48 through 64.**

Practice:

If your son or daughter gets on a team using any of these defenses, you can go back then and practice with them on these drills. Because basically in any *"Zone"* defense, they just rotate around in their area, and seal off. And basically in a *"Man to Man"* defense, they have to stay right with the player they are guarding wherever they move to.

Drill No. 65- The Full Court Press Defense

The Basics are:

This defense is designed to disrupt the opposing teams ability to bring the ball in, and get it up court. In most of the younger age divisions, they have rules that say *"No Press"* allowed in the back court, and 3 feet behind the midcourt line until the opposing team comes into the front court. This is mainly because in the younger divisions, they are more in a training mode. And for a team that is good at it, the full court press can just destroy a teams confidence in bringing the ball up court. And they don't get a chance to learn the game when they keep turning the ball over before they ever get a chance to make a shot. Even so you need to be able to show your son or daughter how it works when they do get on a team, later on, that uses it. It is a very good defensive strategy to use when it is legal to use. The reason is, it is an attacking defense that is very disruptive to a team that hasn't practiced breaking the press.

How it works is when the opposing team brings the ball in at their end of the court, you usually have two guards, or a guard and one forward, get right in front of the players attempting to bring the ball in. One player stands right in front of the out of bounds player , bringing the ball in. They raise their arms, and wave them right in front of that player, and jump up and down in an attempt to grab or knock

FIGURE 107

down their inbound pass *(SEE FIGURE 107)*. The second player attempts to guard the player, trying to catch the inbound pass, tightly, and if possible they try to make a steal.

Practice:

To practice this play you will need one or two helpers. Then you, mom or dad, take the ball and go to a spot out of bounds, at the base line. Or out on the sidewalk in front of the garage. Have your son or daughter get right in front of you, but on the inbound side of the base line. Then they stay right in front of you, waving their arms, trying to knock down or intercept the pass. Have the helper(s) move around behind your son or daughter, and attempt to catch your inbound pass. Remember though mom or dad, you have to stay in the same spot, and try to make the pass to the helper. You can't go running up and down the base line, trying to get free, so you can make the pass. Practice this play a few times until they get the idea of how it works. But don't spend to much time working on it until your son or daughter gets into the upper divisions where the "press" is allowed.

Another way to practice this play is, you can also have your son or daughter tightly guard, and shadow, the loose helper. And attempt to make a steal. However, get another helper to stand in front of you, and wave their arms. On the full court press, the center would usually stay back and closely guard the other center. And the other two players would tightly guard, tightly, the other two opposing players. The *TIP* here is while directly trying to knock down or deflect the inbounds pass, make sure your son or daughter watch only the ball, and not the inbounding players eyes. This way the inbounding player can't head or eye fake them, on where they will throw the pass.

Offensive Drills

Offense is scoring by making baskets. If you don't have a good offense, that can score, you probably won't win the game. Many young kids hardly ever try to shoot a basket, they kind of just stand around and watch. If your son or daughter is at least a little aggressive, they can learn to become a good offensive player. To improve on their offensive skills, you will have to work with them on their dribbling, ball handling, faking, footwork, shooting, passing, and catching. To teach them these skills, you will have to work on them over and over. We have been over how to do this in the section with **Drills 17 thru 47.** What we are going to do in this section is, show you how to teach them the little extra skills for becoming a good offensive player, at the different positions.

Drill No. 66- Guards Moving with the Ball

The Basics are:

Work with them on dribbling, with either hand, over and over. This will improve on their ability to get around the player guarding them. Teach them to be aware of how they are being guarded. That is whether they are being guarded man to man, or if the other team is playing a zone defense. This should be easy for them to figure out. If the player is following them closely where ever they move, then its "man to man". If they are being guarded "man to man", this is what they have to practice doing. When they get close, up court, to a player that is guarding them just to their left, then they dribble with the right hand. And they turn slightly to their right, to use their back and their behind, to shield the opponent from reaching in for the ball. If they see that the player guarding them is moving more to their right, then they need to switch over and dribble with the left hand, turning slightly to their left, to shield off the opponent guarding them.

Practice:

To practice this mom or dad, have your son or daughter take the ball and go out to mid court. Or out on the sidewalk in front of the garage. Then you, mom or dad, go to a spot at the top of the key, or out in front of the basket. Next have your son or daughter start dribbling slowly right towards the basket. Then first you front them slightly to one side, then next time to the other side. Watch them and make sure they switch hands, when they get close, to the side away from you. Let them switch hands though, without reaching in, so they can easily learn this technique. Then when they think they can get around you, have them break away quickly, and dribble drive to the basket. Also make sure they are turning their back to you, to shield you from reaching in to grab or deflect the ball **(SEE FIGURE 108).**

FIGURE 108

Teach your son or daughter to recognize when the other team is in a zone defense, or they are playing way off of them (not guarding them closely) in a man to" man defense". What they need to do then is, dribble in as close as they can to the basket, pull up short, plant their feet, and make a jump shot.

For another practice you can use, have your son or daughter take the ball and go out to mid court. Or out on the sidewalk in front of the garage. Then you, mom or dad, go to a spot about 8 or 10 feet in front of the basket. Then have your son or daughter start dribbling the ball, slowly, towards the basket. Only this time, mom or dad, instead of coming up to guard them closely, back off a little bit. Then give them enough room, to see if they can pull up in front of you and try a jump shot *(SEE FIGURE 67)*. The TIP here is, watch them and make sure they plant both feet solidly, then make their jump shot.

Now we are going to show you how to teach them the "*Screen*", and the "*Pick and Roll*". First the **_SCREEN_**. You will need a helper to work on this play. Both you, and your son or daughter, go back to the same positions as the previous jump shot drill. Have the helper get right behind you. This time, mom or dad, you are going to be the screen person. Have your son or daughter start dribbling right toward the basket. Next you, mom or dad, turn slightly so you can see where the helper is. Then when your son or daughter gets close to you, have them pretend to dribble around to their right (Your left), but then they stop briefly while you screen out (Block) the helper *(SEE FIGURE 93)*. Then have your son or daughter break away around to their left, and drive to the basket for a lay-up. When they have learned how to make this play, then change to the other side of the basket. Reverse everything, and teach them this technique from the other side. This will help them to become an excellent guard. The _TIP_ here is, make sure your son or daughter learns to make the head fake to the right, then change their direction, and their dribble hand quickly, to make their dribble drive.

Now the **_PICK AND ROLL_**. This works just like the screen play, except when your son or daughter breaks to go around, then you fake the screen, let the helper go around behind you, so they can go after your son or daughter. Next you turn and spin roll around, in the opposite direction of where the helper goes, and towards the basket. Now when your son or daughter

FIGURE 109

sees the helper going around behind you, they pass you the ball when you are in the clear, so you can make an easy lay-up *(SEE FIGURE 93 then FIGURE 109)*. Work on these plays, over and over, to get the moves and the timing straightened out. The *TIP* here is, use a little stutter step just before giving the ball back to the screener.

Drill No. 67- Guards Moving without the Ball

The Basics are:

There are a number of things you should teach them how to do without the ball.

1. Teach them to be ready, to screen out an opposing player at any time that the situation presents itself, to help the ball handler to move around freely.
2. Teach them to set up the player guarding them, to run into a screen when the situation presents itself, so you will be free to catch a pass, or move to a spot for a set play.
3. Teach them to keep moving continuously, all around out in the wing areas and high post areas. This so that the player guarding them is kept so busy running all around that they will not be in a position to slide over and double team (Guard) one of your son or daughters team mates.
4. Teach them to get the player guarding them to turn away, and take their eyes off of your son or daughter when the situation presents itself.
5. Teach them to always keep moving around to get open, so they are clear to get a pass from the ball handler. *Don't* just stand around.
6. Teach them to always be ready to get in a position to grab a rebound, or box out an opposing player from getting the rebound.
7. Teach them to always be "thinking" of what the ball handler might be getting ready to do, or what the player that passed you the ball might be planning to do.

Practice:

A. To practice screening out **SEE Drill 66.** The only difference will be that your son or daughter will become the screen person, and you mom or dad become the ball handler.

B. To practice setting up the player guarding your son or daughter you, mom or dad, go to a spot out about 8 or 10 feet in front of the basket. Also you will need a helper for this play. Have the helper stand about 4 or 5 feet to the side of you. Then have your son or daughter go to a spot about 5 feet in front of the helper. It will probably be a good idea to walk them through this first. When everyone is in position, you holler "GO". Then have your son or daughter move quickly towards you, mom or dad. The helper has to try to guard them, and look at them. Your son or daughter has to move in front of you, towards the side away from the helper. When they do this, you stand still and block out (Screen) for them. The helper has to try and stay right in front of your son or daughter, in which case they will run into you. Make sure the helper does what they are supposed to do for the practice because this is for your son or daughters practice, not the helpers. When your son or daughter learns how to do this, then flip flop sides with the helper. This is so your son or daughter can learn how to do this from both sides of you, mom or dad. And remember, all of this is without the ball.

C. To practice continuously moving around, have them get in front of you, out about 8 or 10 feet in front of the basket. Then you, mom or dad, guard them while they keep moving way around, from one wing to the other wing, to get away from you. And again remember this is without the ball. Don't work on this too much, but enough so they get the idea of what to do by continuously moving.

D. To practice getting the player guarding them, to take their eyes off them, will be a little harder. What you will have to explain to them is, maneuver the player guarding them around until that player starts to run into one of your team mates (screener). Then when they take their eyes off your son or daughter, to avoid hitting the screener, your son or daughter has to change directions, and go the other way to get away from them. To practice this, go back to the positions in paragraph B. Then you holler "GO", and have your son or daughter start to move towards you while keeping their eyes on the helper. Then just when the helper takes their eyes off your son or daughter, to avoid hitting them, they change direction and move away from the helper. Don't work on this too much, but enough so they get the idea of what to do.

E. To practice how to keep moving around to get open, go back to the positions in paragraph C. Except you will need a helper for this practice. Then have your son or daughter get in the paint area around the basket, behind the helper while you mom or dad take the ball, and go out to around mid court. Or out on the sidewalk in front of the garage. Next you, mom or dad, take the ball and start to slowly dribble towards the basket, and when you see your son or daughter get in the clear, you make a quick pass to them. The helper has to try and stay right in front of them, and guard them. To get in the clear, your son or daughter will have to keep moving all around from side to side while the helper keeps looking back and forth between you, and your son or daughter. This is a timing play between you, mom or dad, and your son or daughter. So keep working on this, over and over until they have the timing worked out. If they are not catching on as to how to do this, then stop and walk them through it a few times. The *TIP* here is, just when the helper looks back at you, mom or dad, your son or daughter has to be watching the helper, then break away quickly in the opposite direction they were going, so they can catch the pass from you.

F. To practice having them to be ready to get a rebound, or box out, go back to **DRILL 59**.

G. To practice getting them to understand what the ball handler, or the passer, might be thinking , you will have to sit down with them, and show them on a diagram of the court. Explain to them that they have to get to know the ball handlers on their team. And they need to watch, during team practice, to find out where, on the court, the good shooters on the team like to go to make their shot. Then knowing this, what your son or daughter has to do is get into a position to screen out for the shooter. This is so the shooter can get in the clear, to their spot on the court. This is a mental thing, so you will have to start teaching them at an early age, that this is a very important strategy to learn.

Drill No 68- Small Forwards Moving with the Ball

The Basics are:
The small forward needs to practice the same drills as the guard moving with the ball *(SEE DRILL 66)*. There is one other play to work with them on though, that is the "*GIVE & GO*" from the high post area. This is where a player makes a quick pass to a team mate up court, who looks around and waits. Then they shuttle pass the ball back to the player they received it from as that same player runs by, and gets into the clear. The player then dribbles to the basket for a lay-up or a jump shot, whichever is open.

Practice:
To practice this play, you will need a helper. Then have your son or daughter go straight out from the basket, in the high post area at the top of the key *(SEE*

FIGURE 110

FIGURE 1). Next have the helper get in front of them about at the free throw line, and get ready to guard them. Then you, mom or dad, go to a spot out in the right wing area, between the paint and the 3 point arc circle. Next have your son or daughter start dribbling in place for a few seconds as if they are going to stay right where they are. Then all of a sudden, have them make a quick pass to you. Then they break right around to the right of the helper, towards the basket. Then you, mom or dad, wait for a few seconds until they get away from, and clear of, the helper. Then give them a little shuttle pass as they go by. All they have to do then is, catch the pass and drive to the basket fast for a lay-up shot *(SEE FIGURE 110).*

Drill No. 69- Small Forwards Moving without the Ball

The Basics are:
   The "small forward" needs to learn the same basics as the "guard" moving without the ball *(SEE DRILL 67).*

Practice:
   The "small forward" needs to practice the same drills as the "guard" moving without the ball *(SEE DRILL 67)*

Drill No. 70- Power Forward Moving with the Ball

The Basics are:
   The "power forward", moving with the ball, is more like the "center" moving with the ball. This is because in some offenses, the "power forward" plays like a "center" in the low post area. So you will have to teach them the same moves as the "center" moving with the ball *(SEE DRILL 72).* Sometimes though they play in the high post area, so teach them the "GIVE & GO" moves *(SEE DRILL 68 & FIGURE 110).*

Practice:
   The "power forward" needs to practice the same drills as the "center", and the "small forward", moving with the ball *(SEE DRILL 68 & 72)*.

Drill No. 71- Power Forward Moving without the Ball

The Basics are:
   The "power forward" moving without the ball is more like the "center" moving without the ball. For the same reasons as above, they play in the low post area on some offenses. So you will have to teach them the same moves as the "center" moving without the ball *(SEE DRILL 73).* Remember to explain to your son or daughter, they have to <u>get out</u> of the lane (Paint Area) after being in the lane for <u>3 seconds</u>, but only when they are on offense, and their team has the ball. How they can tell when the 3 seconds are up is, when they enter the lane they start counting "One thousand and one, one thousand and two", and so on. On some youth leagues teams, the violation is after 5 seconds in the lane. And a violation in the lane means a turn over, and the other team gets the ball.

Drill No. 72- Center Moving with the Ball

The General Basics are:
   Big tall "centers", moving with the ball, are quite a bit different than "guards", or "small forwards". One of the reasons is, they are usually positioned somewhere around the four corners of the lane (Paint Area). And since they are that close to the basket, they are expected to shoot the ball most of the time in youth leagues. One rule to teach them to remember is, *don't put the ball on the floor* (Dribble) if at all possible. This is because being tall their dribble is higher in the air. And some young centers are not very coordinated, or good at dribbling. What this means is, it gives a smaller, quicker, guard a chance to reach in and steal, or deflect, the ball out of their hands. Teach them to play with their back to the basket, and use their height to their advantage. They have to learn to get both feet planted as quickly as possible when the pass comes into them. The reason is when both feet are planted, and they have their balance, they can pivot off of either foot to immediately go to the basket. There are some special shots, and moves a center needs to learn. They need to learn how to make "the drop step and hook", "the hook", "the power dribble drive", "the turn and square jumper", and "the pump fake and around" shots.

A. Drop Step and Hook Shot

The Specific Basics are:

One way to go to the basket is, the "*Drop Step* and *Hook*" as it is sometimes called. Lets say your son or daughter is on the low post, on the left side of the basket, with their back to the basket when they get the pass. And there is a defensive player right behind them, guarding them. First have them get into the "agressive stance" *(SEE FIGURE 53-A).* What they do next is, take the ball with both hands, and hold it out away from their body towards their left. As if they are going to pass the ball to the left, or move to the left. When they move the ball out that way, and hold that position for afew seconds,most of the time the defensive player will assume they are going to move to their left. So they will naturally lean to their left. When you get them to lean, your son or daughter drops their right foot back a little, and towards the base line. Their left foot becomes the pivot and push off foot. When they do this, your son or daughter has effectively "*hooked*" or blocked the defensive player from moving or reaching around to their right, to stop the move to the basket (This is where the name comes from). Your son or daughters next move is to, pivot on the right foot, swing around with the left foot, to where they are facing the basket. Then all they have to do is jump, and push up a little left handed bank shot into the basket *(SEE FIGURE 111).* If the younger kids can't seem to get this move straight, then stop, stand behind them, and walk them through the footwork a few times, slowly, so they get the feel of it. Then speed it up.

STEP 1   STEP 2

FIGURE 111

Practice:

To practice this technique, have them go to the low post spot, on the left side of the basket. And locate at about 4 or 5 feet in from the base line. You, mom or dad, be the person guarding them. For practice purposes, make sure to leave them enough room to make their drop step. When they have learned this technique, then move to the same location on the other (Right) side of the basket, and reverse the footwork positions for practice on the other side of the basket.

B. Hook Shot

The Specific Basics are:

There is several other moves, you can teach them, off of the above position. The first is the *"Hook"* shot. How this works is, start out at the same position on the low post. Except this time you swing the ball out to the left the same way, then fake the swing around right to face the basket. Next swing pivot around off the left foot the other way (To their left), and take the hook shot over their left shoulder ***(SEE DRILL 43 & FIGURE 80)*** with the right hand and arm. Explain to them that when they are going to take the hook shot, they don't have to take the drop step. It will be a matter of which way is easiest for them, to step and hook, or to just hook. However it's best if they can learn both.

Practice:

To practice this technique, have your son or daughter go to the same spot as in "A" above. Then mix up the drop step and the hook shot, so the defensive player guarding them doesn't know every time which shot they are going to try. On either one of these shots , teach them to get to their position close to the basket on the low post before they get the pass. And close enough so they don't have to dribble, to get to the basket. Practice this on both sides of the basket.

C. Power Dribble Drive Shot

The Specific Basics are:

The third move off the basic position is a power dribble drive to the basket. They would use this move if they are farther out from to basket along the edge of the lane *(SEE FIGURE 1),* about where the "guards" normally are located. How this works is just like the *"Drop Step",* except after the drop step move, and the swing around to face the basket, they start a dribble drive to the basket for a lay-up. They dribble with the left hand when they are to the left side of the basket. And if they are to the right of the basket, they start the dribble with the right hand. This is because they can keep the ball away from the player guarding them, using the shoulder and arm away from the dribble hand.

Practice:

Mom or dad, you can practice this with them by taking the position of the person guarding them. When they have learned this from the left side of the basket, reverse everything and have them practice it from the right side of the basket. If they are not catching on to making this move, then stop and walk them through it several times until they get the feel of the footwork. Again this is where the all the practice on the cross over foot agility drill, and balance, comes in handy. However, remember to explain to them that the power dribble move should only be used when, for some reason, they get the pass and they know they are farther away from the basket than the low post. The *TIP* here is, after they catch the pass, and make the swing move away from the basket, they pull the ball back in *(SEE FIGURE 53-B)*. And they use both hands when they pivot back around to go to the basket. Also have them think "Explode" to the basket, with some speed when they do make the drive to the basket.

D. Turn and Square Jumper

The Specific Basics are:

Here is still one more move, you can teach your son or daughter, off the low post position. That is the "Turn and Square Jumper". This is how it works. When they get the pass in the low post position *(SEE FIGURE 1)*, and they have their back to the basket, they look over their shoulder to see if the player guarding them is back a few feet away from them, instead of up very close. If they are back, they just pivot, turn around quickly, face the basket, jump up, and push up a jump shot *(SEE FIGURE 86 and 92)*. This may not happen to often if your son or daughter is the better player on the team because they will probably be double teamed from front and back. However if you are double teamed and they do give you room, turn and go for the jumper, and if not pass the ball off because a team mate will be open. To make the turn around, teach them to pivot off of the right or the left foot. However, which way to turn will just depend on where the player guarding you is standing. From the left low post if they see that when they turn right, the defender will be right in front of them on their right, then they turn and pivot to the left off the left foot. From the right low post, everything is reversed and just the opposite.

Practice:

Mom or dad, practice this play by acting as the person guarding them. Both of you go to the left low post. Be sure to move side to side, to be in different guarding positions. Like slightly back off behind them, blocking their path to the basket, but leaving them room to turn and shoot. This is so they can practice learning to decide in which direction they need to turn. Also you can teach them to fake the pivot one way, then go the other way. Then reverse or flip flop the positions and work with them on this from the low post on the right side of the basket. It will make them a much better player. If they learn to play from either side of the low post *(SEE FIGURE 1)*, it will make it harder and more confusing, for the opposing team to set up any special plays, to stop them from scoring.

The *TIP* here is, work hard with them on perfecting their quick turn around move, and their head fakes.

E. Pump Fake Around and up Shot
The Specific Basics are:

And here is still another shot you can teach them when they are under the basket, or in the low post areas *(SEE FIGURE 1)*. How this works is, when they catch the ball with their back to the basket, they pivot, turn around and face the basket as in the above drill. Next teach them to move their arms up, holding the ball with both hands as if they are making a jump shot, but they don't let the ball come out of their hands. This move should make the player guarding them jump, up in the air, to block their shot. And when you get them up in the air, you drive around them to the basket for a lay-up shot *(SEE FIGURE 112)*. Again, remember to teach them that if they are double teamed tightly, and can't make the shot, some other team mate is open. So have them look for the open player and pass off the ball.

STEP 1 STEP 2
FIGURE 112

Practice:

To practice this with them, mom or dad, have them go to the low post area first. And next near the the basket *(SEE FIGURE 1)*. Work on this technique from both sides of the basket. Have them fake the shot, with you taking the fake, and jumping up as if to block the shot. However when practicing this technique, make sure to give them room to make the pump fake, and to get around you to the basket. First practice this techniqe from the left low post, then go over and practice it from the right low post area. The *TIP* here is, teach them to make the pump fake as quickly as they can. It's a matter of timing, to get the player guarding them up in the air while their own feet stay on the floor. Otherwise they won't be able to get around the player guarding them.

Drill No. 73- Center Moving without the Ball

The Basics are:

"Centers" moving without the ball is, different from "guards", or "small forwards", moving without the ball. The reason is, they play in the low post, or high post, area most of the time. Make sure you explain to them, and teach them, to not stay in the same place in the zone, for more than 3 seconds. They need to move through, or across, the lane (paint area), or to one of the other four corners of the lane rectangle. Or they move to the free throw line (No. 5), at the high post *(SEE FIGURE 113)*. They must keep moving, so the defense can't set up a play to stop them. This is all so they can get in a clear area, to receive the pass. Remember to point out to them that standing in the lane (paint area), for 3 or 5 seconds, is a violation of the rules, and will cause a turnover. Also explain to them they should be ready to set a screen, or a pick when they move to a new spot. Above all, teach your son or daughter to move around a lot. When I watch some of these young kids play, I see the centers just standing around, and waiting too much.

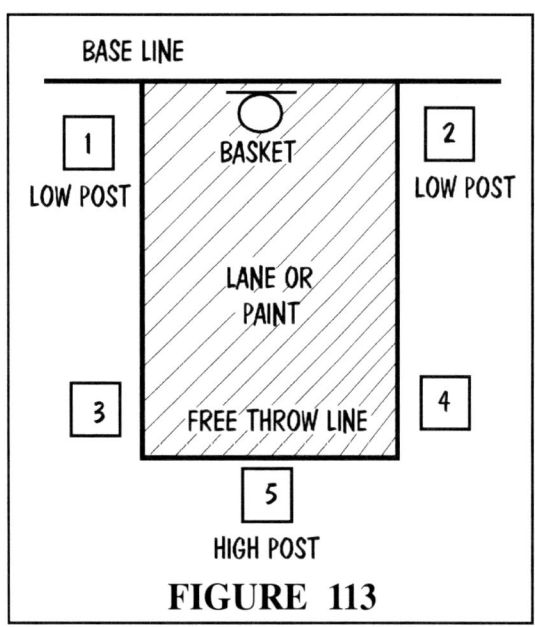

Practice:

To practice this with them, mom or dad, have them start without the ball, at the low post left (No. 1). Then you, mom or dad, guard them sometimes from in front, and sometimes from in back of them. Get them in the habit of counting "One thousand and one, One thousand and two" and so on, to get their timing worked out while in the lane. Then have them quickly move to one of the other four positions, with you mom or dad following them and guarding them. The *TIP* here is, the counting and quickly moving after 3 seconds, in any one spot within the lane.

Other Offensive/ Defensive Strategy Drills

There are other strategy moves, plays, and tactics, that are part of basic basketball as it is played today. You need to teach these to your son or daughter also.

Drill No. 74- Defense During Free Throws

The Basics are:

Your son or daughter needs to understand how to defend after the free throw shot. First thing to explain to them is, they have to stay behind the free throw lane edge line until the ball leaves the free throw shooters hand. If they leave before the shot leaves the shooters hand, the shot does not count, but the shooter gets to try again. The front spot along the edge of the lane, on both sides, goes to a defensive player. Then it alternates with an offensive player, then a defensive player, and so on up to four players along each side of the lane *(SEE FIGURE 114)*. Since the defensive players are closest to the basket, they have to box out the offensive player next to them from grabbing the rebound if the free throw shot misses. By boxing out *(SEE FIGURE 83)* and grabbing the rebound, they get the ball back for their team. Having four players along each side is not mandatory. If the defensive team elects not to put one of its players in the second defensive spot as an example, the offensive (Free throw shooters) team can place one of their players there.

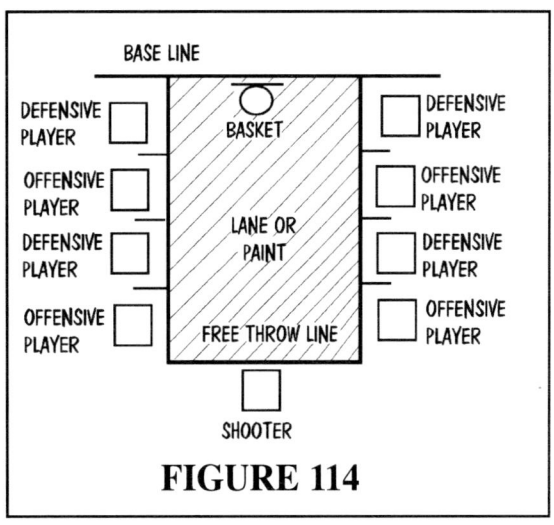

FIGURE 114

Practice:

You will need a helper to practice this play. Then you, mom or dad, take the ball and go to the free throw line. Then have your son or daughter go to the first low post defensive position, and the helper to the offensive position next to them *(SEE FIGURE 114)*. Just as you start to push up your free throw shot, your son or daughter needs bend their knees, and stretches out the arm between them and the helper. This is to get ready to jump into the lane, watch the ball, and box out the helper when the shot leaves your hand *(SEE FIGURE 115)*. However, in some youth basketball leagues, they can't jump into the lane until the ball hits the rim. After you push up your shot, or it hits the rim as the case may be, mom or dad you will have to look over quickly and make sure they did

FIGURE 115 (STEP 2, STEP 1)

not jump out into the lane, before the proper time. And also check to see they "box out" the helper, then jump way up and grab the rebound. The _TIP_ here is, teach them to bend down, and get their arm way out in front of the offensive player next to them. They have to accomplish this without touching the offensive player. Also they have to learn how to use their behind, to keep the offensive player from getting closer to the basket. Again, in some youth leagues, using your behind is illegal also. You will have to check with their coach when they start youth play, to see what the rule is in that particular league.

Drill No. 75- Offense During Free Throws

The Basics are:
When they are the player in the offensive position, along the lane edge line, they have to try and get the rebound away from the defensive player when the shot misses. Also explain to them that if they jump over the line, and out into the lane before the shot leaves the shooters hand, it is a violation. However, in some youth basketball leagues, they can't jump into the lane until the ball hits the rim. And in either case, the shot does not count, and the shooter (Who is on their team) does _not_ get another try. And also explain to them that they can't reach over the defensive players back, and make contact while attempting to grab the rebound. Depending on which way the ball comes off the rim or backboard, it will probably be easier to go around the side of the defensive player, to get to the rebound.

Practice:
To practice this play, you will need a helper. Then all of you go to the same starting positions as in the previous drill 74. Except this time have your son or daughter switch places with the helper, and go to the offensive second lane

space, to start *(SEE FIGURE 114).* When you push up your shot, mom or dad, try to make it bounce off the rim or the backboard, and away from the helper. This way your son or daughter will get practice going around the helper, to get the rebound. And for practice purposes, have the helper always turn their back to your son or daughter, and pretend to box out *(SEE FIGURE 83)* as if your son or daughter is standing right behind them .Even though they know your son or daughter is going to go around them, to attempt to get the rebound. Remember though the practice is for your son or daughter, and not the helper. Work on this from both sides of the low post, to make your son or daughter a better player. The <u>TIP</u> here is, teach them to make a quick fake, going around to the side away from where the ball is going to bounce, then go the other way to the side where it looks like the ball will really bounce.

Drill No. 76- Breaking the Press on Offense

The Basics are:

Another strategy to stop an offense is, the full court press. This is mostly a defensive play. However, you do need to teach your son or daughter the offensive fundamentals of how to break (Get around) the press, when they are on offense. The press starts on the offensive end of the court, with the inbounds pass. I want to point out here that in most of the younger age brackets, in the youth basketball leagues, the press has rules as to when it is allowed. When it's allowed would be in the last few minutes of the game only, or in overtime. Here are some of the strategies to help break the press.

    1. Don't stand right under the basket because if you are the player throwing in a long inbound pass, it might hit the backboard. Stand about halfway between the basket back board, and the side line corner as a starting spot. You are allowed to move back and forth anywhere on the base line, but only as long as it is right after the opposing team has made a basket. On violations or fouls though, you have to stay at the designated spot. Also remember you only have 5 seconds, to get the inbounds pass to your team mate, or you will have to call time out in order for it <u>not</u> to be a violation.

    2. If you see that the full court press is on, and you are a guard or a small forward, look back, then come back to help out if it looks like your team mates will be trapped. By that I mean come back into the back court, to get a pass, or screen an opponent if the press is starting to double team your team mate, who has just caught the inbound pass.

3. Try to screen anyone, of the pressing defenseman, to help your team mate get around the press, then break away to be open for a pass.

4. Try not to get caught with the ball, in the corner of the back court, or get trapped along the side line, with no room to pass over or around the double team.

5. If your team mate gets trapped on the press, with a double team anywhere in the back court, then come back towards him to get the pass. Don't just stand there waiting for a long pass to get to you.

6. When you are dribbling up the court on the press, try not to stop dribbling if at all possible. This leaves you open to getting trapped by the defense when you stop. If you are the ball handler, try to dribble, or get the ball up the court as quickly as possible. The longer you are down in your end of the court, the closer the defense is to their basket, to make a quick score. That is, if they can steal the ball away from you.

7. Always remember to spread out a little, it makes it harder for the defense to trap you.

8. When you see the pressing player starting to come at you, and if you have time, then fake a pass because sometimes it stops their rush to trap you.

9. If a pressing player has their arms way up in the air waving them, remember you can bounce pass the ball under their arms, to get it to your team mate.

Practice:

With all these strategies in mind, here are some ways to practice them. You will need several helpers for this drill. First you, mom or dad, take the ball and go to an out of bounds spot on the base line *(SEE FIGURE 1)*. You should be about halfway between the edge of the basket back board, and the corner of the side line. Or you could go just in front of the garage door, and out a little in front of the basket backboard. Then have your son or daughter go to a spot out in front of you about 8 feet. Next have one of the helpers get right in front of you, mom or dad, and wave their hands to try to block your inbounds pass to your son or daughter *(SEE FIGURE 107)*. Have the second helper guard your son or daughter. What you will have to do is say "GO", then have your son or daughter do a head fake, and move to either side. But preferably to the side in towards the basket, then you try to pass them the ball. I suggest you and your son or daughter both start counting, "One thousand and one" and so on, right after you say "GO", to get your timing worked out on getting the pass to them . Again remember you only have 5 seconds to make the inbounds pass. What this will help them to learn is, how to move quickly to the side to be open for a pass from you. Now you, mom or dad, will have to do some faking. Make the helper in front of you, waving their hands, think you are going to pass to one side. Then out of the corner of your eyes when you see your son or daughter break to the opposite side, then go the other way and pass them the ball. In the mean time, your son or daughter has to break quickly, to get free of the other helper guarding them. If they are "guards", or "small forwards", then work hard on this with them, especially when they are 10 years old, and older. At that age they really need to start learning how to break the press.

Also you can change positions with them, and let them become the inbounds passer, so they will learn how to make the pass without the opposing player making a steal. And when they are an inbound passer, some of the time have them make some long 25 or 30 foot passes to you with the helper in front of them jumping, and waving their arms. This will give them some practice on making the long throw. The *TIP* here is, work hard on the head faking, and remember you can make the short bounce pass under their raised, waving arms. Also remember, you can in some cases move up and down the base line a little bit, to get clear.

Here is another drill you can work on, from these same basic positions. Mom or dad, you will need at least two helpers to work on this play. Have your son or daughter go to the same position in the back court as before with the inbounds pass. Except this time they take the ball, then have the two helpers trap and guard them very tightly, to keep them from passing the ball to you ***(SEE FIGURE 88)***. Then you, mom or dad, get out in front of them about 15 feet, and move around to get in a position to catch their pass. Then say "GO", and the helpers start jumping and waving their arms, to keep your son or daughter from making the pass. Teach your son or daughter to quickly recognize whether the people guarding them are their same size, or taller. This makes a difference because if the players guarding them are the same size, or shorter, they can jump up high, or make a hook shot type pass over the top of them ***(SEE FIGURE 80-C)***. If the players guarding them are taller, they can bounce pass the ball under their raised waving arms. Some coaches like to use a tall center, or power forward, to stand in front of the inbound passer on the press. This is because it makes it harder to pass the ball over them, and it tends to intimidate young shorter players into making a mistake. Again this drill is mostly for "guards", and "small forwards" because most youth coaches use them to inbound the ball. This will be hard for the 5 to 7 year old kids to learn, so keep working with them until they get the techniques mastered. The *TIP* here is, remember to do some head fakes, and get rid of the ball as quickly as possible before the helpers get in close to trap you.

New Parent Orientation

The Game of Basketball

This section is for those mom or dads that may not know much about the game of basketball, or how it is played. The game is played with two teams, each with five players allowed on the court. As in many other sports, the game is divided into two phases. The offensive phase is when the 5 players on a team are bringing the ball up court, by dribbling, or passing, in an attempt to shoot the ball into the basket and score points. The defensive phase is when the 5 players on the opposing team attempt to guard, block, or steal, the ball away from the offensive team, so they can not score points. However, when the defensive team steals the ball away, or there is a turn over (The defensive team gets the ball back), the defensive team becomes the offensive team, and the other team goes on defense. The game is divided into two halves. There are two quarters or periods in a half, then a break, and two more quarters, or periods, to the second half. Making four quarters, or periods, to the whole game. The length of the halftime is about a five minutes, for the players to rest. The length of time for a quarter, or period, is from 6 minutes to 11 minutes, depending on which level of play, or division, the player is in. The teams change baskets, from one end to the other, at the start of every quarter or period. The game is played on a rectangular court, with a basket at each end. In youth basketball leagues, the playing rules may vary a little from league to league, but they basically use high school rules, with their own modifications. The team with the most points wins the game.

The Offensive Game

The Scoring of Points

The object of the offensive team is to get the ball up court, and into their basket to score points. The game is started with a "jump ball" at the center of the court, and also at the start of any overtime, or extra periods, or quarters. At the start of all other quarters or periods, the game starts with the team that has the possession arrow pointing in their favor, bring the ball inbounds from their end of the court. On the jump ball the two tallest, or best, jumpers one from each team, line up in the center circle at mid court *(SEE FIGURE 1),* and face their own basket. The other 4 members of each team are spread out around them in a semicircle usually in alternating positions. The referee takes the ball and gets between the two players, in the center of the circle. Then at their whistle the game starts, and they throw the ball straight up in the air, just high enough to be above the raised outstretched hands of the jumpers. Both players jump up and try to bat or tip the ball, as it is coming down, to one of their own team mates. Which ever team player gets the jump ball, that team then goes on offense with the ball, and the other team goes on defense.

When a player shoots the ball into their own basket and it goes through, and at that same time they are inside of the three point arc line, it counts for two (2) points. If they shoot the ball through the basket, and at that same time they are on the outside of the three point arc line *(SEE FIGURE 1)*, it counts for three (3) points. If they are fouled by a player from the opposing team, they get at least one "Free throw", and maybe one or two more. Which depends on what the situation was when the foul occured. If a legal free throw goes in and through the basket, it counts for one (1) point. I might point out here that free throws can be awarded for reasons other than a foul. Such as when a "Technical" is called against the opposing team. When that happens, your team gets to pick who tries for a free throw. The coach usually appoints your teams best free throw shooter to make the try. Also a basket counts, even though it does not go through the basket, this is if on the shot the referee rules it is "Goaltending" by the defense. "Goaltending" is when an opposing player tips, swats, or knocks the ball away from the basket when it is on the way down from it's flight arc to the basket. It is also "Goaltending" when a defensive player touches the ball while it is above the rim of the basket. If by confusion, or by accident, you shoot the ball and it goes through your opponents basket, the points count for their team.

The Defensive Game

Stopping the Opponents from Scoring

The object of the defensive team is, stop the offensive team from scoring points. When a team goes on defense, they can employ different formations, or alignments, to stop the offense. And as long as these formations, or alignments are ruled legal by the referees, they can be used. As an example, they can play "Man to Man" defense. This is where one defensive player tries to guard an offensive player wherever they go on the court. Or they could employ a "Zone Defense". This is where they form sort of a blocking formation that rotates around towards the side of the court the ball is on. Or they can employ a combination of these two different styles of defense. This is where the state of the art in basketball defense is today.

The defense can employ a full court press defense, to confuse and cause the offense to turn the ball over through steals, intercepted passes, and batting the ball away from an opposing offensive ball handler. In which case the defensive player grabs the ball, then tries to take it to their own basket, to score points. There are basic rules the defense has to follow though. The defense can not foul, hold, or grab, an offensive player attempting to shoot a basket. A foul is basically when the defensive player hits, or grabs, the arm of the offensive player attempting to dribble, or shoot, the ball towards the basket. The defensive player can reach out with their hand and block the ball, or tip it away as long as in the process they do not touch any part of the offensive player. Fouls are also called by the referee when the defensive player reaches, or leans, over the back of an offensive player waiting for a rebound to come down.

Defensive players can stay in the lane or paint area *(SEE FIGURE 1)* as long as they want, so they can block the offensive player from dribbling right down the lane, and attempting to score a basket. The 3 or 5 second violation, in the lane, is not called on the defensive player as it is for an offensive player in the lane. If a defensive player has established a blocking position directly between the offensive player and the basket, the offensive player can not try to drive through, or over the top of, the defensive player. If they do, the referee will call a foul against the offensive player. This type of foul is called "Charging" by the offensive player. There are some alignments the defense can not use because the rules say it gives them an extra advantage. The referee will call this as an "Illegal Defense" violation. I don't think you will see this called very often in the youth leagues though. It mostly happens in professional basketball.

Other Phases of the Game

There are other miscellaneous parts of the youth game that don't necessarily involve the offense or defense. One of these is <u>*time outs*</u>. There are "official scorers" who keep track of the time outs. These people are not part of the team. They are assigned by the league. They record each time out charged, and they keep track of the time during the time out. They notify the coach when their team has reached its 4th charged time out. A team can not take a 5th time out, or they are charged with a penalty. Scorers have an official clock, and a stopwatch, for keeping track of the time outs. They will sound a warning signal (Usually a horn of some kind) 15 seconds before the end of the charged time out.

The official scorer will record how many *fouls* each player receives. When a player reaches their 5th personal foul, they can not play any longer, and they are out of the remainder of the game. They also record *technical* fouls. A technical foul can be a foul by a non player, a non contact foul by a player, or an intentional or flagrant contact foul while the ball is dead. Two *Direct Technical* fouls on any player or coach will result in their ejection, and possible indefinite suspension, from all activities.

No *jewelry* or *earrings* are allowed in most youth leagues, even if covered by tape. This is for the protection of both the offensive and defensive players. If a religious medal is allowed to be worn, it must be taped to the body, under the uniform. Leagues may allow a *head band* to be worn if it meets the following criteria:
1. If it is prescribed by a medical physician.
2. If it is not abrasive, hard, or dangerous to another player.
3. It is attached in such a way that it is unlikely to come off during the game.
4. It is no wider than 2 inches.

There can be "substitutions" during the game. However, they must report to the scorers table, then wait for the referee to motion for them to enter the game. When a substitute player enters the game, a player on that team must leave the court, but not the game. They can be a substitute player that will re-enter the game later on. Also they must give the scorer their number, and the number of the player who is being replaced. Such as "I am Mary Sue number 5 coming in to replace number 16 Angela Hill".

The Playing Rules

Basically the rules say each team shall have 5 players on the court. Most youth teams follow High School rules that have been slightly modified, for the benefit of the younger kids just starting out. Each team starts out with a basket to defend. What that means is, they line up around that basket, and try to keep the opposing team from shooting the ball through that basket. The game starts with a "jump ball" at center court. The team that gains control of the jump ball goes on offense, and tries to shoot the ball through their basket. If they make the basket the defending team takes the ball out, at their own base line, and throws it in to one of their own players. At which time they go on offense, move down the court, and try to shoot the ball through their basket, located at the other end of the court. Once the offensive team moves down the court, and past center court, they have a certain amount of time to take their shot at the basket. This is sometimes referred to in the professional game as "The 24 second Clock". This length of time is about 35 seconds in college basketball. In the youth basketball leagues it is not used most of the time. This is probably because they want to give the younger players more time, to get into a position to attempt a shot. When a non shooting foul (No free throw is awarded) occurs, in most cases, the team that had their player fouled takes the ball out on the side line. They take it out at the spot where the foul occurred. The game officials keep track of a "_Possession arrow_". What the arrow determines is, which team gets the ball, to make a throw in to one of their team mates. Every time a team makes a throw in, on a possession arrow, the officials keep track of who takes the ball out next, by changing the direction the possession arrow points. Then next time the other team gets to throw the ball in. Actually though it doesn't make any difference who makes the foul, the team with the arrow pointing towards their basket makes the throw in.

There are different kind of _Fouls_. Generally speaking, if a player hits the arm of an opposing player, attempting to shoot or move the ball towards the basket, grabs them, or blocks them, in an attempt to stop them from moving the ball, then a foul is called on that player. The player that has been fouled gets to take one, or more, free throws. If the foul is a technical foul, player control foul, a non-shooting type foul such as traveling, or two opposing players holding the ball at the same time, then the ball goes out to the side line. The possession arrow determining which team gets the ball. The reason I am mentioning this is, many times as a parent in the stands you will hear a whistle blow, and the game stops. And you probably wonder what happened. Well most of the time it is because a foul has occurred. Some times you will hear a loud horn device go off. This is the official scorers way of signaling the referee, or it could be the official timer making a warning signal, or signaling the end of time for each quarter.

How the Players Line Up

The players will line up around the basket in many different ways, depending on how their coach wants them to play defense, or offense. For some of the more typical line ups, and alignments **SEE FIGURE 1 & 2.**

Makeup of Teams

Boys and girls Youth Basketball Teams have been broken up into many different divisions as you go all over the United States. The following will give you some idea of what division level your son or daughter might play in, and what size ball to use *(ALSO SEE FIGURE 118)*.

2ND thru 5th GRADE DIVISIONS:

Boys and girls ages 8 to 11 years. They all use the smaller 18 to 20 ounce,

28 ½ inch (Women's) circumference Ball.
6th thru 10th GRADE DIVISIONS:
Boys ages 12 to 16 use the 20 to 22 ounce, 29 ½ inch circumference ball.
Girls ages 12 to 13 use the 18 to 20 ounce, 28 ½ inch (Women's) circumference ball.

The Court Size

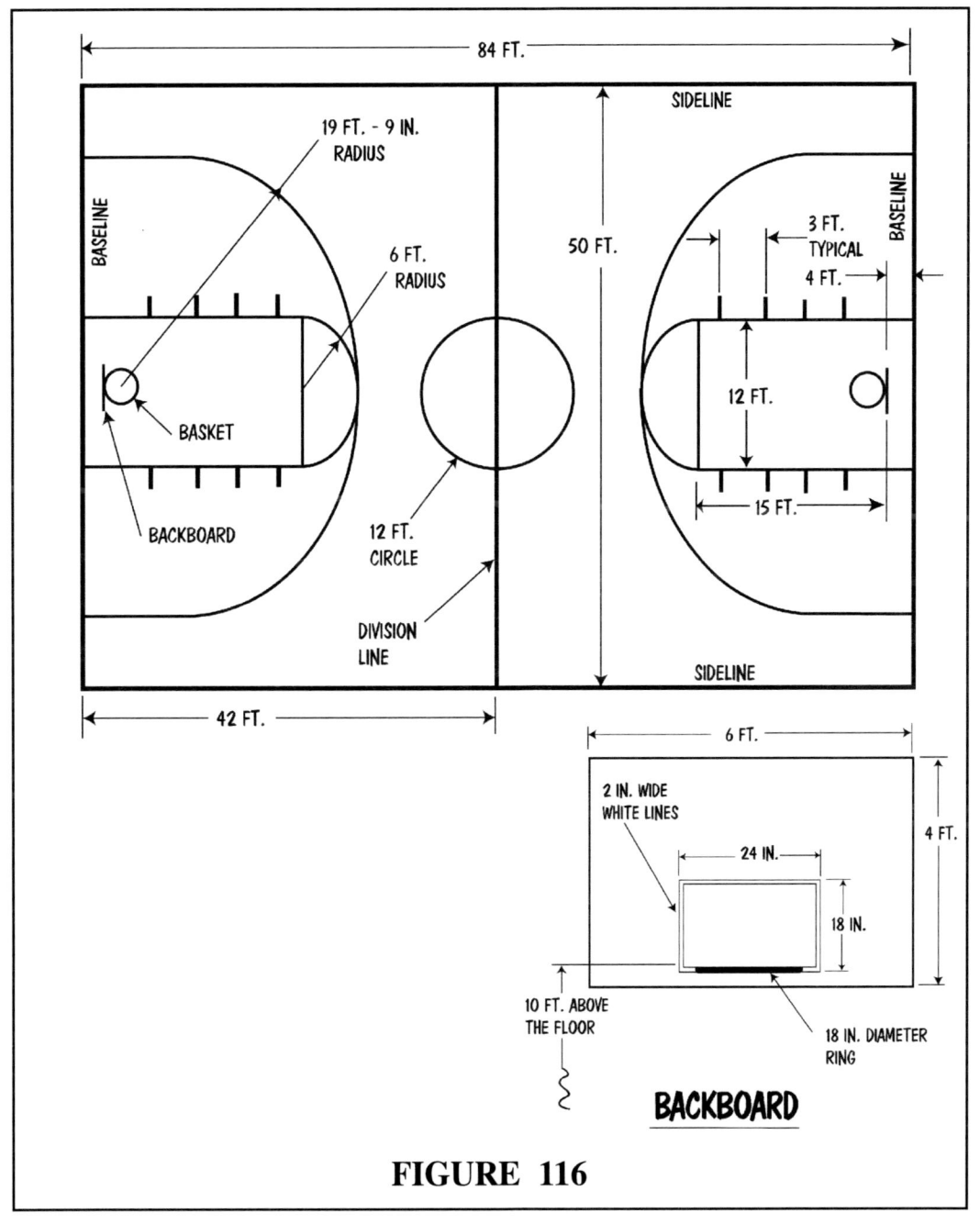

FIGURE 116

The court size will vary a little bit from each level of play, such as college, and professional, all the way to the youth leagues. This is because it is sized to fit the smaller boys and girls. The size shown is basically the ideal youth size *(SEE FIGURE 116)*. But some youth courts may vary from this a little bit. Most of the time it just depends on which court is available for the game to be played on.

The Referee's

Why we have Referee's

I think it is very obvious, without them the game could get out of hand and arguments, disagreements, fights, fan rioting, and who knows what else might

FIGURE 117

happen. Basketball games have referees to control the game, make sure the rules are followed, to make it fair for everyone. The game of basketball is more complex than most parents realize, and that is why we need these people there to keep track of all these rules. The Referees are assisted by an *official Scorer*, and a *Timer*. The Scorer, and Timer, are located at a table at the side of the court.

What they Do

At most youth games there will be a Referee and a umpire, or a referee and two umpires if they can get them. The Referee basically has authority over the umpires(s) on decisions, except on calling a foul. The uniform of the referee and umpire is a black and white striped shirt. The referees and umpires have signals for fouls, and other infractions of the rules. For these signals see **FIGURE 117**.

Equipment

In each level or division of Basketball, they basically have the same uniform. They have to wear a jersey, or tee shirt, and shorts that stay above the knees. They should wear socks, "tennis" shoes, or flat rubber soled athletic shoes, for better traction on the wood floors of the court *(SEE FIGURE 119)*. Most Youth Basketball Leagues follow the "National Federation of High School" rules. Distinctive uniforms are required. This basically means the uniforms of each team can not be just alike, they have to have different colors or shades such as black and white, or light and dark, to make it easy for everyone to determine which players are on each team. The home team is required to make a change, to accomplish the distinction if necessary.

Basketball is a simple game as far as equipment is concerned. The only other item you need besides the uniform is a basketball. For sizes there are two *(SEE FIGURE 118)*. And for practice the only other thing you need is, a backboard with a basket.

In Youth Leagues players can only wear a protective guards on their elbow, wrist, knee, hand, forearm, or finger if they are all soft, and the

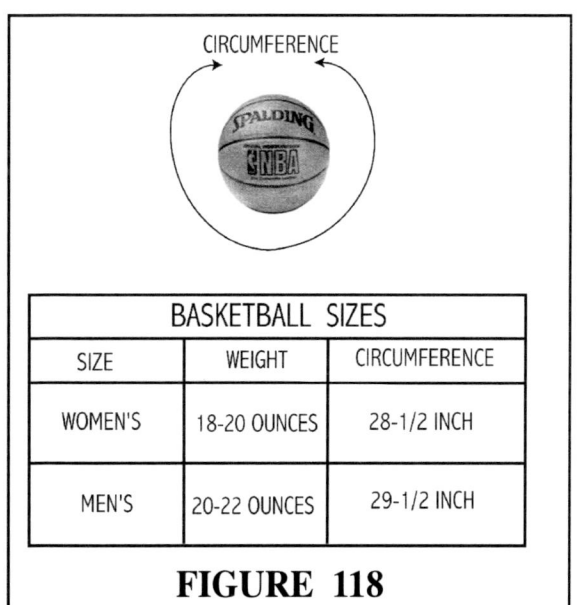

FIGURE 118

referee approves them. *"Ankle Braces" are* usually not mentioned in most Rule Books, but if your son or daughter has a good reason, or a doctors permission, the referee will probably allow it. For wearing earrings or jewelry see the section on *"Other Phases of the Game"*. *Mouth Guards* are a good idea to use, to help protect the teeth, mouth, and tongue. *Athletic Supporters and Cups* are for boys, to protect the groin area.

It's probably also a good idea to get a *Ball Inflator*, to keep the ball fully inflated, so it doesn't go flat. And some of the newer basketballs have a special deflation valve feature now. You will also need a special needle valve adapter tool that fits into the basketball.

You can find most of the equipment at your local sporting goods, or athletic equipment store. However if you have a computer, you can find all of the different types of equipment on the *"INTERNET"*.

FIGURE 119

Try these other excellent books for teaching your Son or Daughter sports Fundamentals.

Teach'in Football - Teach your son all the basic fundamentals he needs, to play the game of football. Mom and dad, you will have fun teaching him, and he will have more fun playing the game because he will feel like he knows what he is doing. This book is complete with everything both of you need to know. It covers all the positions, new parent orientation to football, equipment required, field size, and game rules.
ISBN 0-9705827-4-9, soft cover paperback, 8 x 10-1/2, 138 pages.

Teach'in Baseball & Softball - Teach your son or daughter all the basic fundamentals they need, to play the game of baseball or softball, and all in one book. Mom and dad, you will have fun teaching them, and they will have more fun playing the game because they will feel like they know what they are doing. This book is complete with everything both of you need to know. It covers all the positions, new parent orientation to the game, equipment required, field size, and game rules.
ISBN 0-9705827-2-2, soft cover paper back, 8 x 10-1/2, 161 pages.

These books and other Jacobob Press Ltd. books are available from your local bookstore, or by calling the supplier at (314) 843-4829.

Index

1-3-1 Zone Defense.........................117
2-3 Zone Defense 113, 117
24 Second Clock 141

A

Agility Drills..............................25
Ankle Brace 145, 146
Athletic Supporter.......................... 146
Attitude Development....................9

B

Back Extension Drill....................29
Backboard 143, 146
Ball, Holding the............................76
Ball Inflator 146
Ball Inflator Tool 146
Ball, Release, Follow through..............80
Ball Sizes..................................145
Baseline 18
Basket 18, 146
Basketball, Defensive....................139
Basketball, Offensive....................138
Basketball, Playing Rules 141
Basketball, Referees Signals 144
Basketball, sizes 142, 143
Basketball, the Game of 138
Blocking Shots 107
Books, Other Sports............................146
Box & One Defense 118
Boxing Out 95
Braces, Body Parts........................145, 146

C

Catching the Ball.............................62
Center Circle 18
Center, Basics..........103-108, 116, 127-132
Centers (General) 13
Charging Foul 102, 116, 117, 140
Coordination Drills 25
Court, size 143, 144
Crossover Foot Drill........................25
Cuts, making..............................70

D

Defense, Free Throws 133
Defense, Man to Man......96 thru 112
Defense, The Game of 139
Defense, Zone ....113 thru 119
Defensive Stance.................................92
Defensive Techniques 96
Diseases, Infectious Control............12
Diving for the Ball 112
Dribbling (General) 45
Drills, Ball Handling...........................48
    Behind the Back........................52
    Change of Pace............................61
    Dribbling Techniques...............48
    Fast High Speed...........................48
    Low Speed..................................50
    Shuffle.....................................58
    Spin Move...................................56
    Stop and Go...............................59
    Stutter Step................................50
    Switch Hands Crossover..............53
    Through the Legs......................54
Drills, Catching................................62
    Toughen the Hands.....................62
    Catching the Ball........................62
Drills, Coordination/ Agility................25
    Crossover Foot............................25
    Running Backwards....................26
Drills, Defensive 96
    Centers in Zone Defense............116
    Forwards in Zone Defense.........115
    Full Court Press Defense.........119
    Gen. Diving for the Ball............112
    General Shot Blocking 107
    Guards in Zone Defense.............113
    Making Steals 108
    Man to Man Center 103
    Man to Man Guards Converge.....99
    Man to Man Guards Rotate 98
    Man to Man Point Guard............96
    Man to Man Power Fwd............101
    Man to Man Rebounding...........110
    Man to Man Screens 105
    Man to Man Shooting Guard......97
    Man to Man Small Fwd.............100
    Rebound/Steals in Zone Def......117
Drills, Dribbling..................................45

    Basic Dribble..........................45
    Eithger Hand..........................47
    No Look..................................46
Drills, Faking..................................64
    Offensive Faking....................64
    Defensive Faking...................66
Drills, Footwork.............................68
    Ready Stance.........................69
    Making Cuts...........................70
    Making Pivots.........................71
    Making a Jump Stop...............72
Drills, General.....................................19
Drills, Guarding.............................92
    Boxing Out..............................95
    Defensive Stance....................92
    Shuffle Slide Side Step............94
Drills, How do they help.................19
Drills, Jumping..............................73
    Grab the Flag.........................74
    Over the Broomstick..............73
Drills, Offensive...........................120
    Center Moving with Ball........127
    Center Moving w/o Ball.........132
    Guards Moving with Ball.........121
    Guards Moving w/o Ball.........123
    Pwr Fwd Moving w/ Ball........126
    Pwr. Fwd Moving w/o Ball.....127
    Sm Fwd Moving w/ Ball.........125
    Sm Fwd Moving w/o Ball.......126
Drills, Other Off/Def Strategy...........132
    Breaking Press on Offense......135
    Def During Free Throws.......133
    Off During Free Throws.....134
Drills, Passing..............................40
    Both Hands Bounce Pass..........41
    Both Hands Chest Pass............40
    Both Hands Overhead Pass......42
    One Handed Pass...................43
Drills, Running.............................37
    Speed Burst Running..............38
    Wind Sprint Ladders..............37
Drills, Shooting............................75
    Body Mechanics...................77
    Free Throw Shots...................87
    Holding the Ball.....................76
    Hook Shots.............................89
    Jump Shots............................86
    Lay-Up Shots.........................83
    Release, Follow Thru, Arc.........80
    Shooting Mechanics................78
    Shooting Stance......................77
    Three Point Shots..................91
    Tip In Shots............................88
Drills, Strength............................27
    Abdominal Slide.....................35
    Back Extension.......................29
    Biceps Curl.............................33
    Chest Press.............................30
    Dumbbell Rowing..................28
    Shoulder Front Raise..............32
    Shoulder Shrug......................31
    Sit Up Crunches.....................34
    Straight Leg Dead Lift.............29
    Toe Raise................................36
    Wall Sits.................................36
    Wrist Curl..............................32
Drop Step...128

E

Earrings..141
Equipment..............................145, 146
Equipment, InterNet.......................146
Exercises..19
Exercises, Warm up/Stretch.............19
    Ankle Stretch..........................24
    Back Stretch............................21
    Butterfly Groin Stretch...........20
    Kneeling Thigh Stretch..........22
    Lats & Postier Del Stretch.........23
    Neck Stretch...........................24
    Pelvic Twist Stretch................22
    Seated Leg Stretch..................20
    Side Lunge Stretch................21
    Standing Calf Stretch............23
    Trunk Twister.........................20
    Wrist Stretch..........................24

F

Faking..64
Footwork..68
Forward, basics.......100-102, 115, 125-127

Forwards, Power (General)....................16
Forwards, Small (General)....................15
Fouls 141, 142, 145
Fouls, Personal 141
Fouls, Technical 141
Free Throw Line 18
Free Throws 87, 133, 134, 139
Free Throw Strategy Drills...................133
Full Court Press 119, 135, 140
Fundamentals 12

G
Gator Aid......................................12
Getting Open 124
Give & Go Play 125
Goaltending 107, 139
Grab the Rim 88
Grade Divisions, Players.............142, 143
Guarding 92
Guard, Basics.............96-99, 113, 121-125
Guards, Body Parts............................146
Guards, Point (General)....................14
Guards, Shooting (general).................15

H
Head Band 141, 146
Health Habits 11
Held Ball 108, 109
Hesitate Step Move............................50
High Post Area 18
Hook Shots..............................89, 129
Horn 140, 142
Hustle 10

I
Improving 9
Inbound Pass.................119, 120, 135-137
Inbound Pass, Time of.......................135
Inflator, Ball..................................146
Influence on 9

J
Jewelry 141
Jump Ball 138, 139, 141
Jumping 73
Jump Shots....................................86

Jump Stop.....................................72

L
Lane 18
Lie on the Back Drill..........................81
Line, Free Throw 18
Loose Balls, Diving for 112
Low Post Area 18

M
Man to Man Defenses ....96 thru 111
Mechanics, Body..............................77
Mechanics, Shooting..........................78
Mouth Guards 146
Moving with the Ball ....121 thru 131
Moving w/o the Ball............123 thru 132

N
New Parent Orientation 138

O
Offense, The Game of 138
Offense, On Free Throws 134
Offensive Techniques ....120 thru 137
Official Scorer 140, 141
Organize your Teaching.......................17
Orientation, New Parents 138
Other Phases of the Game 140
Out of Bounds Swats 110

P
Pick and Rolls 122
Paint Area 18
Pass, Bounce 41
Pass, Chest 40
Pass, Inbounds 119, 120, 135-137
Pass, Overhead 42
Passing (General) 40
Pivots, making................................71
Players, how they line up...................142
Players, where they line up 18
Points, Scoring 138, 139
Possession Arrow 142
Power Dribble................................129
Press, Breaking on Offense 135-137
Press, Full Court 119, 135, 140

Protective Guards. 145, 146
Pump Fake Around & Up......................131
Putting Ball on Floor 127

Q

Quickness 38

R

Ready Stance......................................69
Rebounding 74, 110, 117
Referees 9, 144
Referees, what they do 145
Referees, why we have 144
Referees Signals 144
Respect 10
Rotating 98, 99
Rules, Playing 141
Running 37, 38

S

Scoring Points 138, 139
Scoring, Stop Opponents from.............139
Screens 105, 106, 122
Sealing Off 116
Shoes 145, 146
Shot Blocking, General 107, 108
Shots, Bank In 83, 84, 128
Shots, Dribble Drive.......... 48-50, 84-86
Shots, Drop Step 128
Shots, Free Throw 87
Shots, Hook 89, 129
Shots, How much time 141
Shots, How to hold Ball 76
Shots, Jump 78-82, 86
Shots, Lay-Up ....83 thru 86
Shots, Pwr Dribble Drive...........48-50, 129
Shots, Pump Fake and Around & Up.....131
Shots, Tip In 88
Shots, Three Point 91
Shots, Turn & Square Jump.................130
Shooting..75
Shooting Stance..................................77
Shuffle Side Step Move......................94
Sidelines 18
Signals, Referees 144

Sit on the Chair Drill..............................81
Socks....................................145, 146
Steals 108-110, 117
Strength (General).............................27
Strength, Abdominals 34
Strength, Arms 32
Strength, Chest 30
Strength, Legs, toes, ankles..................36
Strength, Lower Back 29
Strength, Shoulders 31
Strength, Thighs...............................36
Strength, Upper Back 28
Stretching 19
Stutter Step Move..............................50
Substitutions 141
Switches 105, 106

T

Teams, Make up of 142, 143
Technical Foul..................................141
Technical Foul, Direct........................141
Thinking, Teach them..................76, 123
Three Point Shot's..............................91
Time Out..140
Toughen the Hand's............................62
Turn & Square Jumper........................130
Triangle & 2 Defense 118

U

Uniforms 145, 146

W

Warm Ups 19
Warnings...6
Where they play on the court............17, 18
Wing Area 18
Wrist Guards 145, 146

Z

Zone Defenses..................95, 113 thru 119